# NOT ALL ROADS LEAD TO GOLD

A path of persistence, faith and perseverance

## 2X OLYMPIAN JIM GRUENWALD
### WITH CRAIG SESKER

**NOT ALL ROADS
LEAD TO GOLD**

**A path of persistence,
faith and perseverance**

**By Two-time Olympian Jim Gruenwald**
With Craig Sesker

Copyright: 2022 Jim Gruenwald
Edited by Nancy Newhoff
Photos by Larry Slater, Tony Rotundo
Cover design by Ben Strandberg
Published by Kingery Printing
Designed by Angie Hardenbrook
Cost: $25.00

No part of this book may be reproduced or transmitted in any form or by any means, electronic or mechanical, including photocopying, recording, or by any information storage and retrieval system, without permission in writing from the publisher.

Printed in the United States of America

First Edition

# FOREWORD

### By Tom Ryan
*NCAA championship coach*
*Ohio State University*

Hope you are ready for a glorious and mind-blowing journey that will lead you exactly where all meaningful stories go. To the truth. To the laws and principles of excellence and personal growth that were established long ago. And will always stand the test of time.

They are irrefutable. They are enlightening. And they are hard. They are filled with God's carefully crafted message for us.

The simple and undeniable reality is that there is no choice more sustainable or powerful than true love. Love has the capability to bring us on an unrelenting ride toward our most lofty goals, sustain us through pain, settle us through disappointments and great loss while bringing our deepest purposes to life.

This is a love story in its truest sense. The love of a man for his craft, his community, his God and his family. A man who picked up responsibilities regardless of their weight and carried them. He held on to the burdens he said he wanted, and in the process, he taught us all a whole lot of something special.

I have been blessed to get to know Jim Gruenwald. He's

# NOT ALL ROADS LEAD TO GOLD

authentic. The closer I get and the more I learn about him and from him, the more I am drawn to him. He's a normal man with perfect love. A man who's unrelenting "will" and love led him down a road that brought him incredible growth and insight.

In the pages of this book, you will walk alongside Jim, witness his perseverance and experience his painful setbacks. But most importantly, you will come to learn that winning isn't everything and that countless blessings come in the journey. The journey to become. And the journey to become even more.

As a World Class wrestler, things didn't happen overnight for Jim. His progress was typical of truth – not the truth of this world. He painstakingly made gains day after day, practice after practice, and year after year. It wasn't easy, but it was worth it. Nothing Jim has done or anyone else has done of any high regard is easy. That's the point. The hard stuff keeps us coming back.

It's a noble cause to shoot high. Jim's aim was extremely high and he gave it his full attention. He poured his life into winning World and Olympic gold medals. Being the No. 1 man in the World at his weight class was his aim. Those around him knew it. There was no compromise. In the pages ahead, you will learn far more about life than winning.

Ordinary people can do extraordinary things when they deeply pursue what they love.

# CHAPTER 1
# MAN OF THE HOUSE

It wasn't supposed to be this way. I was sitting on the driveway, listening to my dad. I was a little kid thinking little kid thoughts. My parents were getting a divorce. I was sad, distraught, scared and confused. I was just six years old and I had already experienced plenty in my short lifetime. I had a fairly tumultuous early childhood. But it was the only life I knew.

That life began when I was born on June 9, 1970 in Milwaukee, Wisconsin, the state's largest city with a population of 600,000 people. Milwaukee is located in southeastern Wisconsin on the western shore of Lake Michigan.

At my first official weigh-in, I tipped the scales at 6 pounds, 9 ounces. I also like to think I was my dad Gary's favorite birthday present since we share a birthday.

My dad worked as a plate engraver for 40 years at the Milwaukee Journal newspaper before retiring. My mom, Diane, worked long hours as a typesetter and later as a print press operator for several different companies.

My brother, Alan, was born a year after me. We lived in a suburb of Milwaukee called Oak Creek.

The further you get from your childhood, the less you remember – except for the big moments. There were plenty of memories – good and bad – from my formative years. We would grill hot dogs, brats, and hamburgers with my grandparents. And we would swim in a small kiddy pool in the summer. One time a

## NOT ALL ROADS LEAD TO GOLD

neighborhood kid was throwing rocks and caught me in the side of my head – that sent me screaming, bleeding and running inside our house. On another occasion, I decided to ride a Big Wheel down the basement stairs. And my brother and I spent our share of time re-enacting scenes from the Three Stooges.

But the most vivid memory came when my dad walked me outside our house, sat me down on the driveway and looked directly into my eyes.

"Jim, you're going to have to be the man of the house now."

It's a day that I will never forget. Even today, the thought makes me tear up a bit. That's tough for someone that young to hear. And it was pretty traumatic for a 6-year-old to see his dad walk away and not really know or comprehend why. My dad meant well, but those are words that a parent should never tell a kid that young.

My parents argued, but so did Al and I. The difference was that adult arguments make kids uncomfortable in a way the kid arguments don't. Sneaking out of bed, peeking around a corner, and seeing the fight that leaves you scared and scarred. As a kid, hearing them makes you want to hide under the covers.

My parents finalized their divorce when I was 7. The one positive that came out of it was that my brother and I didn't have to see or hear our parents arguing anymore. When my dad moved out, the tension in the house was gone.

Believe it or not, my parents actually got along great after they divorced. I do not recall a single time either said anything bad about the other after they split up. I don't remember a single argument after the divorce. There was the occasional tension over shared holidays, but what kid doesn't want two Christmases or two Thanksgivings – well, until we started wrestling.

After my father left, Al and I didn't see him that much initially. I saw him maybe one weekend a month and was around him for a few weeks in the summer.

I do recall some fun moments when we did see him. We played basketball and miniature golf and went to an occasional movie at the drive-in theater.

*A path of persistence, faith and perseverance*

We would swim in the pool at my dad's apartment. He would throw us in the pool – until the day Al and I were able to throw him. But there wasn't much of the deeper quality father-son time.

Like almost every kid who grows up in Wisconsin, you are exposed to three professional sports teams – the Green Bay Packers, the Milwaukee Brewers and the Milwaukee Bucks. The Packers are a historic and storied franchise that has one of the most passionate fan bases in all of sports.

My dad loved and was a die-hard fan of all three teams. I watched because he watched. My response was to start playing sports – basketball in fifth and sixth grade, baseball in seventh grade, and football in ninth grade.

None of them held my interest, partly because I was tiny and as I got older, my vision started becoming worse. I was near-sighted and the problem wasn't fixed until my sophomore year in high school.

The only sport that really appealed to me was wrestling. Weight classes are an amazing thing for small kids that struggle to compete in tall or big man sports.

My dad didn't initially follow my wrestling. He was still a fun weekend dad, but it was challenging to forge a relationship because we simply weren't together that much.

And as you grow from little kid to middle schooler, you start asking questions. What happened? Why doesn't dad come to my games or matches?

I started questioning my mom, and I learned the main reason my parents split up was because my dad was an alcoholic. He had serious drinking issues and my mom just couldn't take it anymore. She knew it wasn't a healthy situation and environment for our family, especially with me and my brother being so young. Something had to change and eventually it did with him leaving and my parents getting a divorce.

My dad wasn't a hard liquor alcoholic, more of a "beer-oholic." He would sit and watch his favorite team on television and drink beer. He would think about his childhood. As a 9-year-old boy, he watched as his 5-year-old sister was tragically killed in a drunken driving accident. Yet he still drank. He would respond to the hard moments with beer. He would hang out with his buddies and drink beer.

Between the divorce, the time apart and the limited time together, my emotions were conflicted. I don't believe I hated my father when I was growing up, but I'm not sure I loved him. It was a confusing time for someone so young. We spent so much time apart and this was the norm until about two years later when I started wrestling.

The other part of the equation was watching my mom struggle, at first in her marriage, and then as a single parent. It was difficult for her. She was ostracized by her family because they were strong Catholics and divorce was frowned upon strongly by her religion. She knew going into the marriage that if there were marital problems there was no going home.

My mom and dad were broken people trying to put the shattered pieces of their lives back together. The kids are collateral damage in a divorce and it was difficult for everyone.

My mom worked her butt off to support our family. I admired her greatly for that. She worked 60 to 80 hours a week to support us. I know she did everything she could to provide for all of us. My dad also did his part and paid child support, but he was living in an apartment. With his own expenses, he didn't have much extra money to spare.

Long hours of work leave little time for housework, so my mother made a list of chores for me and my brother. If we did the chores, she at times left some change for a treat. If we didn't do our chores, we typically would receive a spanking. My mom had a pink bath brush she used to paddle our butts. It was made out of hard plastic and was a great reminder and motivator for us to have everything done and done well.

The spankings were definitely old-school discipline. My mom was small in stature, but she could still bring the heat. She was only 4-foot-11 and 90 pounds, but it felt like we were getting spanked by a 1,000-pound gorilla. We were never abused, and

*A path of persistence, faith and perseverance*

looking back I appreciate the discipline and the skills developed doing housework. The older I get the more I appreciate what my mother suffered through and endured in those years after the divorce.

The spankings were a deterrent to a degree, but I would still land in my share of trouble. My brother and I were a handful when we were growing up. We were two out of control kids with a lot of freedom because our mom worked crazy hours. My mom did everything she could to keep us in line. She was a tough disciplinarian, and that's exactly what I needed when I was that age.

One time I got in trouble and my stepdad grabbed the brush and started to spank me. A large crack followed and the brush shattered on my butt. It was a huge moment. My brother and I experienced the bath brush quite a few times – and they were all deserved. That was the end of an era – the bath brush was broken.

If it were not for that early discipline, wrestling and Jesus, I would be in prison. I really believe that. I was a troublemaker and I was headed down the wrong path.

There was a softer side to discipline earlier on. I remember stealing some Chapstick from a convenience store when I was really young. I was right around 6 years old and I just grabbed the Chapstick out of a box when we were inside the store. My mom immediately figured it out when I was walking out the door of the store. She saw I had something in my hand and asked me what it was. She made me take it back and apologize.

But as my brother and I aged a bit and crept closer to the pre-teen years, we started fighting a lot. We would break things. We did things kids who were that young and that close in age would do. We would get grounded and then sneak out of the house when my mom was at work. We couldn't fool her though. She would call the house, and if we didn't answer, we would be in trouble when she got home. She always knew when something was going on – even if she wasn't there.

My mom eventually got remarried and that was another big

## NOT ALL ROADS LEAD TO GOLD

life change. We didn't handle the transition very well. My brother and I were disrespectful to my stepdad.

Our stepfather, Bill, must have really loved my mom to get roped into our family. Al and I were feisty, strong-willed and hypercompetitive. I know that's typical for brothers to act that way, but we were pretty rambunctious.

I have always been a bit of a goofball. My brother and I liked re-enacting the Three Stooges, a show that involved a lot of physical comedy where they would playfully smack each other on the head. I liked to mess with my brother the way those guys did when we watched them on TV. What would start out as a fun skit would then lead to one of us hitting the other too hard. That would lead to retaliation and eventually World War III.

My parents did the best they could trying to make the best out of our situation. But it wasn't easy. Especially with two mischievous boys who had an abundance of energy.

With our parents working long hours, and with limited supervision, the situation was a terrible combination and often a recipe for disaster.

I was always small in stature growing up – the story of my life. I would become super frustrated in school because I was one of the smallest kids in my class. What I lacked in size, I tried making up for in personality. I was always fighting for attention and wanting to be noticed by the teachers. I always had my hand up in class.

I remember moving a lot during my childhood, and bouncing from one school to another. When my mom got remarried, we moved to the little town of North Prairie, Wisconsin. It was located about a 45-minute drive from where we had been living. We settled there for four years.

After we moved, my brother and I quickly made friends in our new neighborhood. But we didn't always get along with everybody. As is typical with kids, you go from best friends to a fight to best friends in a span of five minutes.

One day at the bus stop, Al and I got into a fight with a kid named John Boetcher. He was a big kid compared to us, but that

*A path of persistence, faith and perseverance*

described just about everybody. He weighed around 100 pounds and I was a scrawny little guy who weighed 60 pounds. We were in sixth grade. Despite him being much bigger and stronger than I was, I didn't back down from him. A quick three punches to his face, and he was bent over crying. Thinking the fight over, I let my guard down. He responded by double-legging me and tackling me to the ground. His dad broke up the fight and he was the one in trouble – one of the few benefits to being small.

Later that year, we were back to being friends and he asked me if I wanted to come to wrestling practice. Remembering that bus stop moment made for an easy yes.

I joined the wrestling team as a sixth-grader. Our team only practiced for six weeks and I learned some basic techniques and had a chance to wrestle live in practice. After the six-week program, I ended up having one match that I lost 3-2. Even though I was new to wrestling, and it was my first match, I was still pissed off. I didn't like to lose. At anything.

With my dad's love of Wisconsin professional sports and my mom trying to find an outlet for my aggression and energy, I was one of those kids who was in a gazillion different sports. In addition to wrestling, I played football, basketball, baseball and soccer.

In fifth and sixth grade. I was the starting point guard on the basketball team. I wasn't great at basketball, but I was small and fast. And I could pass and dribble. By seventh and eighth grade, the other kids kept growing and I barely did. My basketball career was short-lived.

Being competitive has a tendency to drive risk-taking. I was pretty fearless, and my brother and I did our share of crazy and dumb things when we were home.

I remember jumping off the roof of our house and the garage. We would challenge each other to see how high we could jump from. It was one of those stupid things that kids do, but I didn't want to lose to anybody. No matter what we were doing.

Al and I were only a year apart, but most people thought we were twins. Despite being younger, by the time middle school

## NOT ALL ROADS LEAD TO GOLD

arrived he was bigger, stronger and a better athlete than me. This added another level of frustration and tension.

Growing up, when things went sideways, I would become frustrated and angry. I saw that with my parents with the way they would angrily react to situations. They had some struggles and we saw that frustration. As my mom navigated the waters of single parenthood – long hours, low wages, and lack of sleep – she would become frustrated and angry. As kids, you learn behavior from your parents, but the behavior is always magnified by youth and immaturity.

My mom was struggling back then, and she was doing the best she could. On her day off, we would go to the International House of Pancakes and get the 99-cent Smiley face chocolate chip pancakes. One order was big enough to feed the three us.

Like my mother, I had a quick, explosive temper and I could lose control of my emotions in the blink of an eye. I would become enraged and pissed off. I would blow off steam and then be done with it. The rage never lasted long, but it wasn't a good habit. I would get super angry and then be fine a couple of minutes later. Well, until the next time.

I wasn't intense all of the time. I also enjoyed having fun and goofing around. But I was serious and ultra-competitive when I played sports. My one advantage over my brother was my competitiveness. A switch would flip when I was in a competitive setting, and I would become very serious and intense. It was a wonderful quality that served me well in wrestling, but pre-wrestling it just led to fights.

As the fighting between my brother and I continued to escalate, my mother sought outside help. It became so bad that my mom eventually went to see a psychologist. And he made a recommendation. His brilliant idea was we should be permitted to fight for 10 supervised minutes a day and then would not be able to fight at any other time of the day. By doing that, the psychologist believed it would get the fighting out of our system. The only extra rule my mom imposed was that we weren't allowed to punch each other in the face during the 10 minutes and

## A path of persistence, faith and perseverance

then we were supposed to be done.

The problem came when my mom would leave and go to work. Alan and I would start talking about the 10-minute fight we were allowed to have and get into a real fight about who won. The introduction of the 10-minute fight actually led to more fighting.

Wrestling was the perfect outlet for someone like me who was fearless, aggressive and had an abundance of energy. I loved the combat aspect of it. I could fight, within the framework of wrestling rules, and not get in trouble. There were weight classes and I could actually match up against kids my own size. I loved the idea of that.

I came back for my second year of wrestling in seventh grade and made some improvement. We wrestled a handful of matches that season and I was learning more techniques.

The following year is when wrestling starting to become a bigger deal for me. I started to become more serious about the sport. I went 12-0 in eighth grade while wrestling on my middle school team as an 80-pounder.

After the eighth-grade season I had my first introduction to Freestyle wrestling that spring. Freestyle is an international style of wrestling used in the Olympic Games that was different from the Folkstyle used in middle school, high school and college. Freestyle matches were wrestled almost exclusively on your feet with opponents looking to take each other down.

I entered my first Freestyle tournament feeling pretty good because I went undefeated for my middle school team. But the reality of being a big fish in a small pond became evident in my Freestyle debut. I wrestled twice and lost by technical fall and was pinned. I got destroyed. In one of the matches, I became so frustrated that I punched a kid in the face. It was in the heat of the moment, and I didn't react well to losing.

My behavior and response to losing needed to change. I had also become a Christian, but was new to my faith. After receiving some advice, I learned to find a quiet dark place and release the emotions of loss.

Any time I lost, from when I was a little kid until I was an

## NOT ALL ROADS LEAD TO GOLD

Olympian, I would go somewhere quiet and cry. The pain of losing hurt so much I needed a release. I always cried after losing, but now I did it without punching someone in the face or losing control publicly. The crying was cathartic and would allow me to hit the reset button and come back strong.

After the horrible first tournament, I came back really determined to master my next Freestyle matches in eighth grade. I absolutely hate losing. I hate losing more than I like winning. I was driven to be successful. The emotions of winning are so brief in my eyes. The emotional high doesn't last long because you are always looking ahead to the next match. You remember the losses. I don't remember as many of the wins – I remember the setbacks because they are so painful. It hurts – it hurts deep.

You train so hard for something and leave it all on the line and you come up short. Or a guy crushes you and you realize you're not as close to your goals as you think. You have to hit the reset button when you lose – you can't let it define you because it's soul crushing. It provides direction. The lines are sharper and it's more defined.

The one major benefit of losing is that it provides clear direction on what you need to fix and what you need to work on. Was I not in good enough condition or was my technique not as good as it needed to be? You are looking for answers to those questions. Was I coming up short in the top or bottom position, or on my feet?

Winning or losing do not define you – it directs you. One of the things that shackles athletes is a fear of losing. When an athlete truly embraces the battle, it frees them up to wrestle better. Win or lose, you can still walk off the mat with your head held high. It still hurts to lose, but if you wrestle freely, you can maximize your performance.

I didn't know all of that back then obviously, but I definitely learned from my setbacks and I ended my eighth-grade Freestyle season by winning the Wisconsin state title at 80 pounds. I was a member of the Oconomowoc Wrestling Club. It wasn't an easy name to spell or pronounce, but it was a great club to wrestle for.

## A path of persistence, faith and perseverance

We had practices two or three times a week during the spring. I was just wrestling Freestyle then. I didn't wrestle the other Olympic style of Greco-Roman until my freshman year of high school.

Greco-Roman is the classic Olympic style of wrestling that has roots in Ancient Greece. The Greco-Roman style is all upper body wrestling where you can't attack your opponent's legs. Wrestlers score points in Greco-Roman by throwing, lifting and turning their opponents.

Winning the Wisconsin state title was a pretty cool accomplishment for me. It was exciting and my parents were happy to see me having success.

My mom's way of encouraging me was always to look at my opponent and then tell me my arms were bigger. She would look at the guy I was wrestling and if my arms were bigger than my opponent's arms, she was confident I could beat the other guy. I was a skinny little kid, and there were at least one or two kids below me on the podium who had bigger arms than me. I'm sure that helped my mom feel better when I walked out there to compete.

That was my first state championship at any level of wrestling and obviously I was super excited. It validated what I was doing and made me hungry to accomplish bigger goals. I qualified for the regional tournament with kids from other Midwestern states. My pond was getting bigger – I was a big fish in my state but now I was moving to the regional level against tougher competition.

After winning the Wisconsin state Freestyle title in 1984, I went to the Northern Plains Regional. I finished fifth in the regional tournament in Bismarck, North Dakota. That was a significant improvement and prepared me for the next level – high school wrestling.

## CHAPTER 2
# BELIEVE AND ACHIEVE

Before I started my high school wrestling career, I did what most of my friends decided to do. I gave football a try. Being a "massive" 90 pounds dripping wet, I ended up being the third-string running back on the freshman B team. I liked football, but I was tiny and I was terrible. I finished the season, but that was the only year of football I played in high school.

Wrestling was the sport I was focused on now and I had high expectations when I began practice as a prep freshman in 1984. I wanted to be a varsity starter as a freshman and qualify for the Wisconsin state high school tournament.

Unfortunately, the lowest weight class in high school was 98 pounds and I was going to be undersized as a freshman. I always wanted to be bigger and stronger. I only weighed 90 pounds, meaning I could eat all I wanted. And I could also put on muscle. I loved lifting weights. I was trying to add size and strength so I wouldn't be overpowered by my bigger opponents who weighed as much as 120 pounds in the offseason.

Between growth and lifting, I was able to get closer. I remember the excitement of being close to 98 pounds by the end of the season.

Even though I had been successful as an eighth-grader, I began my freshman season on the junior varsity for Mukwonago High School.

## NOT ALL ROADS LEAD TO GOLD

Competing as an undersized wrestler was challenging, but one advantage I did have was that I wasn't sucked down or worn out from cutting weight. I always had plenty of energy because I didn't have to reduce my calorie intake to make weight.

I landed on the junior varsity because our team had a senior on the varsity at 98. He beat me solidly when we wrestled off for the varsity spot – he crushed me.

What I remembered most about that kid was something that had nothing to do with wrestling. He had a unique ability where he could touch the tip of his nose with his tongue. That was an impressive feat.

My career as a junior varsity wrestler was short-lived. We moved midway through my freshman year and I transferred to Greendale High School.

The transition occurred during some tough times for our family when we were struggling financially. My stepdad, Bill, lost his job and interest rates were in double digits for mortgages. I didn't understand any of this at the time, but I remember begging my mom and Bill not to move. Moving halfway through my freshman year of high school left me feeling empty, scared, and angry. For the first time in my life, I felt like we had established roots and settled down. Moving sucked and I obviously wasn't happy about it.

The moving didn't stop, and we moved a handful of times when I was in high school and college. Fortunately, my mom realized the importance of keeping us in the same school district for the next few years.

Moving to a new school district is challenging, especially midway through the year. Friend groups are already established, some from elementary and middle school. Mukwonago was a rural community. Greendale was an upper middle-class community and I felt like the poor square trying to fit into the round hole.

Mukwonago had a huge wrestling team – varsity, junior varsity, and underclassman squads. Greendale had a varsity and some extras. Wrestling was popular at Mukwonago and at

### *A path of persistence, faith and perseverance*

Greendale we seemed unwanted.

When I transferred to Greendale, I quickly learned that one of my teammates, senior Brett Bekken, was a big fan of popular rock and roll star Bruce Springsteen. Brett was one of the best wrestlers on our squad. He was team captain, qualified for state for the second time, and finished with a 25-2 record at 155 pounds that season.

During one of my first days at Greendale, Brett approached me before practice, and in an off-hand way asked, "What do you think of Bruce Springsteen?"

Not knowing his deep love of Springsteen, I ignorantly and naively replied, "I don't know who he is. I don't think I like him." That was a bad response. I was the new guy in school and that was the exact wrong thing to say.

Brett outweighed me by 60 pounds. He grabbed me and then proceeded to hog-tie me with my jock strap. In that moment, I was changing clothes for practice. The jock strap was my sole piece of clothing. He then carried me over and dumped me on the ground in front of the girls' locker room.

What I didn't realize was that it was about a minute before the girls started basketball practice. Despite frantic efforts to untie myself, with my arms and legs secured behind my back, the unknown became known. The girls on the team walked out of the locker room and saw me on the ground.

Too horrified and embarrassed to even ask for help, which I doubt was forthcoming, I managed to untie myself eventually amid the sounds of laughter and disgust.

That was the only time that guy ever really picked on me. There was never any intense bullying or hazing. But my teammate obviously wanted to send me a message that day.

Maybe it was Brett's way of "welcoming" me to the wrestling team. I don't know. It only happened once. I do know one thing. I never became a Bruce Springsteen fan.

During my freshman year, there was another incident that happened to me at my high school but not related to the wrestling team.

## NOT ALL ROADS LEAD TO GOLD

One of my classmates came up to me from behind and knocked the books out of my hands. We were both using a shortcut through the teachers' parking lot from auto shop class to a main hallway. My books went flying and the papers inside the books went flying. And then my temper went flying. The rare type of temper where you really do see red.

Not realizing I was a wrestler, he singled me out as small and weak and an easy target. The smirk on his face made it immediately apparent he did it on purpose.

After he knocked the books out of my hands, there was a moment of shock. My calm turned to rage. And the smirk on his face turned the rage into the fire of a thousand suns. I looked at him and I said, "That was really f---ing stupid." I rarely used profanity, but I was beyond rage. And I swore at him.

He wound up and took a swing at me. Wrestling instinct answered in a heartbeat. I grabbed his arm mid-punch, did an arm-drag, pulled him close, grabbed his throat, and slammed him against the hood of a car. And I just kept squeezing. And squeezing. And squeezing.

Frantically squirming, he managed to get his feet on the bumper and with the height advantage was able to push out of my grasp and run away.

A few minutes later, I was called into the principal's office. They asked me what happened, and fortunately for me a teacher had witnessed the incident and came to my defense.

There were no other major incidents. And eventually the move to Greendale was beneficial for my wrestling career.

I ended up having a good freshman season on the mat for Greendale High School. I achieved one of my goals by qualifying for the Wisconsin state high school tournament.

Going to state for the first time was an awesome, memorable and eye-opening experience. The state tournament was held in this huge arena at the University of Wisconsin in Madison and it was filled with 10,000 cheering fans from all over the state. The place seemed massive to me. And like many freshmen, I had never wrestled in a venue that size.

## *A path of persistence, faith and perseverance*

I was a small kid in the lightest weight class, looking around with giant saucer eyes in this gigantic arena. And it was a little overwhelming and intimidating.

I had more anxiety than eagerness. I was a 14-year-old kid who had never competed in front of a crowd of that size and it showed.

I'm not sure exactly how much it affected or impacted me, but I walked out on the mat for the first match of my first state tournament and fell flat on my face.

I was tight, tense and nervous, and I didn't wrestle well. I ended up choking pretty badly and losing the match 5-3. I gave up two takedowns and that was the difference in the match. Then the guy who beat me lost his next match and I was eliminated from the tournament.

I was frustrated because I should have won that match. I knew I was better than the kid who beat me. I had lost in the first round at the state tournament. I was still only a freshman and undersized, but that is small consolation when I had lost a match that I knew I should have won.

I had a successful season with a 20-6-1 record, but I wanted more. That setback drove me and motivated me to become more successful.

When I arrived at Greendale, one of the first people I met was Bob Carlson. He was the head wrestling coach at Greendale High School and also my freshman English teacher. Coach Carlson was a good coach who had his own unique ways of trying to push and motivate us.

On the way to the state tournament in Madison, we rode in his car. He put in a cassette tape and cranked up the volume. At the time I had no idea it was a Billy Ocean song, but the lyrics stuck, "When the going gets tough, the tough get going."

When I first heard the song, I didn't quite understand the lyrics. I was a young, naïve kid, but I eventually figured out what it meant. Regardless, I let it fire me up to battle through adversity and perform my best under the most challenging circumstances.

Coach Carlson wasn't an overly dynamic coach or very

## NOT ALL ROADS LEAD TO GOLD

boisterous. He wasn't a loud coach and didn't yell a lot, but he could be intense. He looked like an athlete. And looked like a wrestler. He stood 5-foot-10, and he was a strong guy with big arms and a big chest. He was a solid coach with a solid understanding of the wrestling. He loved coaching and loved his athletes. He pointed me and my brother in the right direction as high school wrestlers. He was the right coach at the right time. He had a significant impact on me as a mentor. He cared about us and wanted the very best for us.

Watching him coach successful and unsuccessful wrestlers, I realized his care for us was genuine. He wasn't a transactional coach that only cared when you won.

As I became better in the sport and started to gain accolades, Coach Carlson asked me to help with some of the instruction in practice. He had me show techniques to the team. I appreciated the opportunity to do that and help our guys. Looking back, I gained a better understanding of wrestling by teaching.

And I was more than happy to try and help some of the younger guys on our team. I enjoyed teaching and providing instruction, and that would serve me well later in life.

Following my freshman year of high school, I jumped back into the international styles of wrestling in the spring.

When we moved from Mukwonago to Greendale, my dad started coming to all of my events. I distinctly remember his excitement as he watched near the mat. He slapped the mat as I pinned my opponent in the finals of Sectionals, our state qualifying event.

Wrestling became the sport that bonded our family. After my freshman season, my dad really started becoming involved with my wrestling. He would look up tournaments and take me and my brother to events. It was awesome seeing him develop an interest in what we were doing.

As my dad became much more involved in my wrestling, we had a chance to spend more time with him. This time also allowed him to become more involved in my life. My dad became a fixture supporting us in the stands. That enabled my brother and

## A path of persistence, faith and perseverance

I to form a stronger relationship with him.

He never tried to tell us how to wrestle or what to do in a match, and that was great because he hadn't wrestled himself. He left the coaching to our coaches. Yes, he understood the basics, but he actually never became a student of the sport. What he did do was cheer for us and support us. And drive us to tournaments and help financially with the costs to travel to events. That was the best way he could have approached it and it worked well for us. It was great having him more involved in my life.

My father still battled the same demons. Al and I knew he drank, but I don't recall him losing control around us in high school or college. Looking back, I get the sense that wrestling helped to fill the void that beer often did. He eventually stopped drinking and has been dry for more than 20 years. I'm very proud of him for that.

That spring and summer, I won Wisconsin state titles in Freestyle and Greco-Roman wrestling for all age groups. I went on to win the Northern Plains Regional Nationals at the Cadet level (14-16 years old) in Greco and freestyle at 99 pounds.

I was excelling in both Olympic styles of wrestling and that was encouraging for me. Competing in different styles enabled me to become a more complete wrestler.

By the time my sophomore season rolled around at Greendale High, I had experienced a growth spurt. I was roughly 25 pounds bigger than I was the previous season.

But I decided to compete in the same weight class. I wrestled in the 98-pound division for the second straight season. It wasn't easy. Looking back, maybe it wasn't the wisest move either.

After being an undersized 90-pounder as a freshman, my natural weight was now around 115 pounds. I already was pretty lean and had a low percentage of body fat, so the cut down to 98 was brutal at times.

I would starve myself and then I would binge eat. I would dehydrate myself and lose water weight. It wasn't the healthiest or smartest diet plan, but I was a young 15-year-old kid who

## NOT ALL ROADS LEAD TO GOLD

didn't know any better. I didn't have much guidance when it came to weight management.

In the middle of my sophomore year, we were in between places because our rent had been raised and my mother informed me that we needed to move. We lived with a friend of my mother for a short period of time until we could find an affordable apartment.

One night, I was hungry and decided to make a pizza. I put a cheese pizza in the oven. When I looked inside to check on the crust, I saw something dropping on top of it. And it wasn't black olives. I wasn't sure what it was at first and then I discovered there were cockroaches on the pizza.

You couldn't throw it away because we didn't have much money then. I was hungry so I still ate the pizza, sans the cockroaches.

One night, I was hungry, cold and going crazy. I just needed to get out of the house. Grabbing some of my summer job money, I went to a movie theater and watched Rocky IV. It was an inspirational boxing movie where Rocky Balboa traveled to Russia and overcame adversity to battle Ivan Drago in his home country in front of a hostile crowd.

It was great motivation, for a few hours anyway. I didn't enjoy it as long as I would have liked. I was sitting in a theater by myself, I was hungry and I was miserable from cutting so much weight.

There wasn't much weight management oversight. There were no hydration tests or weight management calculators or body composition regulations. There was just cutting weight. It was an ugly part of the sport that didn't get addressed until the late 1990s. I just did what everyone who I knew did. I starved myself and worked out. I thought was the best and only way to make it down to 98 pounds.

By the end of my sophomore year, I was jaundiced, and I had lost much of my muscle mass. Even with the huge toll weight-cutting had taken on me, I made it back to the state tournament.

## *A path of persistence, faith and perseverance*

This time, I wasn't intimidated or overwhelmed by the big arena in Madison. And I didn't lose in the first round this time.

I won my first match. And my second. And then my third bout. I was on a roll and my confidence continued to grow. I had reached the championship match of the Wisconsin state high school wrestling tournament.

A year after being negatively impacted by the massive arena and larger-than-life atmosphere at the University of Wisconsin, I felt right at home during my second trip to state.

I was undefeated and ready to achieve my goal of being a state champion. I carried a perfect 28-0 record into the 98-pound state finals.

My opponent was Ron Pieper of Stoughton. I came out strong and took the lead, but then something went wrong. Terribly wrong.

I was winning the match and I went foggy – I don't really know what exactly happened. I don't remember if I was choked or thrown on my head, but I remember being confused at the time.

I ended up losing the match by an 8-4 score. I don't even remember being upset or angry after I lost the match. And that didn't make sense because I always got mad when I lost.

I'm not sure if I suffered a concussion or what exactly happened. It was a puzzling, troubling and frustrating way to end my sophomore season.

I finished the season 28-1 and placed second in the state. Standing on the medal podium was a surreal feeling. I had made significant improvements, but I still fell short of my goal.

You rarely see a second-place finisher with a smile on their face. It's great to place so high, but it's crushing to be so close and not win the championship you so badly covet. As a 15-year-old, that wasn't easy to process. My dad's consoling words did help a bit:

"Son, there are hundreds of kids that would love to trade places with you and only one wrestler you want to trade places with."

## NOT ALL ROADS LEAD TO GOLD

Now that the high school season was over, I was smart enough to realize that I needed a break. I took some much-needed time off after the state tournament.

I was never someone who took many breaks from training. But the massive weight cut and the tough setback in the state finals had taken a huge toll on me. My body and my mind needed time to recover from a stressful season.

I did make one decision at that point. I vowed never to cut that much weight again. My mom threatened to kick me out of the apartment because no one wanted to deal with five months of 'Hangry Jim.' I bravely vowed never to cut that much weight again and avoided my mother's wrath.

After my sophomore season in high school, I hit the weight room hard. The time off from wrestling was refreshing and allowed me to hit the reset button and come back strong in the spring.

I won Cadet State Greco and Freestyle Championships. I won the Northern Plains Regional Nationals in Freestyle and Greco-Roman at 112 pounds.

The Freestyle and Greco State tournaments were the qualifying events for both the Junior Nationals and, in 1986, the first USA Wrestling Cadet National Tournament held in Grand Rapids, Michigan.

I won the Cadet Nationals Greco-Roman title at 112 pounds. I had captured my first national title. Winning a national title in Greco was awesome, but I didn't have much time to celebrate with Freestyle starting the next day. USA Wrestling didn't give out the big stop sign plaques that they do now. It was just a regular plaque, but it was still super exciting to win my first national title.

The results were not as good in Freestyle, but I still placed fourth at Cadet Nationals after winning a title in Greco.

I was starting to have better results in Greco-Roman wrestling even though I didn't practice or compete much in that style. We wrestled Folkstyle all winter during the high school season before switching to Greco and Freestyle in the spring and summer. I

## *A path of persistence, faith and perseverance*

didn't have access to spring and summer club wrestling. The training was just the weight room and Saturday tournaments.

The highlight of every summer was the Junior Nationals. I dropped down to 105.5 pounds for that event. Despite my earlier success, the Junior Nationals was an open event to anyone still in high school.

I did manage to place seventh, which wasn't a bad achievement for my second time at Junior Nationals. The only two guys I lost to finished first and second. The losses were still annoying, and I didn't get a chance to wrestle anyone who placed 3-6. What made the losses even more frustrating were the scores of the bouts.

I lost 14-14 on criteria to the first-place finisher, and I had the second-place finisher on his back at the end of the match after smashing him in a headlock. I was only 16 years old, and most of my opponents were 17 and 18. I walked away feeling good about how I wrestled, and I knew I wasn't that far away from beating the best Juniors in the country.

Considering my only wrestling training was the weeklong camp before Junior Nationals, I had made another significant jump with my wrestling during the summer after my sophomore year of high school.

It was definitely another step up the ladder and a huge confidence boost for the next high school season.

Even though I had excelled on the national level in the summer, I still hadn't won that elusive Wisconsin state high school championship.

I came back for my junior season on a mission to capture my first state title. I had cut too much weight the previous season, and I elected to move up two weight classes to 112 pounds as a junior. I was very comfortable at that weight class, and the late summer and fall weightlifting added some additional muscle.

I wasn't miserable and wasn't always worried about how much I weighed. I had more energy for practices and meets. I wasn't training just to lose weight: I was training to get better.

I felt much better, but I still suffered a setback during the

# NOT ALL ROADS LEAD TO GOLD

early part of my junior season against a talented wrestler named Chris Scott, who competed for West Allis Nathan Hale High School.

A three-time conference champion by his senior year, Chris was "the man" in our conference. He was a tough wrestler and he was winning everything.

I faced Chris in the third match of the season, and he beat me 5-3. I started the match a little bit tentative and starstruck before I realized that I could actually beat him. I definitely put Chris on a higher pedestal than I should have. Granted, he was a senior and I was a junior. Chris had won our conference three times, but I had finished second at state the year before. I should not have lost.

When the match ended, I pounded the mat in frustration after I lost. A lady from our church, Carol Burt, was there watching me and she saw how I reacted. She scolded me a little when I saw her. She reminded me that I represent something greater than myself, and it wasn't very Christ-like for me to react like I did. I didn't want people to think I was out of control with my emotions and that's how it looked with my reaction to losing that match.

I was a Christian at that point. My conversion happened in seventh grade. After Carol talked to me, it made me think about my actions. The optics of it were terrible that I was losing control about a wrestling match in front of a crowd of people. I learned from it.

Coach Carlson took a more practical approach and told me that I should have used that energy in the match rather than anger after the match.

Later that season, I had an opportunity to avenge that loss to Chris Scott in the finals of the conference tournament.

Chris was trying to make history and win his fourth conference title, but I was determined to prevent that from happening.

I reversed the outcome from earlier in the season and beat Chris 6-0 in the conference finals. The pedestal was gone and the

## *A path of persistence, faith and perseverance*

idolization was replaced by determination. I came out aggressively and I took him down and turned him to his back. I was a hammer on top in that match. I had a pretty nasty arm bar and rode him effectively one period and got an escape in another.

It turned out the early season loss to Chris Scott would be my only setback of the season. Chris and I met again in the state semifinals and I earned a hard-fought 2-0 victory. Chris was determined to avenge the loss to me from the conference finals and our third match of the season was a tough battle.

I scored a takedown in the first period and rode him out for a 2-0 lead in the first. He rode me out in the second period, and I rode him out in the third period. It was a super close match. We had three guys from our conference place at state in my weight class of 112 pounds that season. We were in Class A, the biggest class in Wisconsin.

I advanced to the state finals for the second straight year. And I would face the same opponent – Ron Pieper – who had defeated me in the championship match the year before.

This time, I wasn't in a fog. I came out focused and determined. And ready to complete my season-long mission of winning a state championship.

I wrestled one of the best matches of my prep career. I charged out strong and built an early lead. Pieper became frustrated when he fell behind and head-butted me. I immediately responded with a headlock to take a 10-0 lead before eventually winning the match by a 10-2 score.

It was a tough, brutal, physical match. When time ran out and the match ended, I jumped with my hands in the air to celebrate as the crowd cheered.

My mouth was bleeding when the match ended, but that didn't matter. I had finally won and was crowned the 1987 Wisconsin high school Class A state champion at 112 pounds.

I hugged my coaches and then found my parents in the stands to share an emotional hug with them. I remember being super excited. Winning state was a huge deal and it was a goal that I had been pursuing for a while.

## NOT ALL ROADS LEAD TO GOLD

I finished with a 31-1 record in my junior season. And I had come back to earn two wins over the guy, Chris Scott, who had defeated me early in the season. And I avenged my state finals loss from the previous year.

As with any fulfilled goal, it was gratifying to know that the long hours of training and years of sacrifice had finally paid off for me. It had been quite a journey for a kid who just a few years back was headed down the wrong path in life.

Wrestling is a big deal in the state of Wisconsin and there have been several elite wrestlers who have come out of my home state.

So winning state was a prestigious honor that carried a great deal of significance. I was joining an exclusive group of athletes when I became a Wisconsin state champion.

I wasn't the only Gruenwald in the state finals that year. My brother, Alan, took second at state at 119 pounds in 1987. He was a sophomore. Our team had a losing dual-meet record that season, but our team finished sixth at the state tournament because we had a champion and a runner-up finisher with some early bonus points.

I entered the Greco-Roman and Freestyle season on a huge high after winning a state high school title, and I captured state titles again in Greco and Freestyle before setting my sights on Junior Nationals.

I wrestled 11 matches over two days en route to finishing third at the Junior Nationals in Greco-Roman. I won nine matches, including three by fall and three by technical fall. Unfortunately, I lost to the top two placers again.

My goals were becoming bigger. And for the first time, I started thinking about a goal I would pursue for a number of years that followed.

I first started thinking about wrestling in the Olympic Games when I was in high school. I had a conversation with my mom and I told her, "I want to be an Olympic champion." She was totally on board with it. She knew I had already won a national championship in my age group as a Cadet, and I was

*A path of persistence, faith and perseverance*

getting closer to winning another title as a Junior. The Olympics was no longer something that was totally unrealistic or far-fetched.

My mother held me to a high standard, on and off the mat. My dad was enjoying the ride and my mom wanted me to mash the gas pedal. Neither of my parents were around a lot, but each added a needed quality.

My dad had the quiet encouragement and support. My mother often challenged and demanded me to do my best. She wasn't in my face. She would ask questions and probe, and try to help you get to the place where you wanted to be. She was trying to help me reach my goals and she encouraged me to pursue them.

My mother wasn't around home that much because she was working 60 to 80 hours a week. She did so much to support our family. Even though she couldn't attend most of my competitions because she was working, she was in my corner 100 percent. When she talked, I was listening.

She wasn't the most subtle in her approach, but her message still got through. She knew I wanted to be the best and she felt like it was something I could achieve.

Before I could think much about my newly launched Olympic dream, I still had a year left of high school.

I bumped up one weight class to 119 pounds for my senior season at Greendale High School. I was a returning state champion and a two-time finalist, but nothing was going to be easy during the 1987-88 scholastic season.

When the season started, there were four state champions in my weight class. That group included me, Ron Pieper, Dennis Hall of Hartford and Jeff Bubolz of Wisconsin Rapids.

Bubolz had defeated my brother the year before in the 119-pound state finals. Dennis had moved down a weight class. I moved up a weight class and Ron moved up.

During the season, Ron Pieper moved up one more class to 126 pounds and it paid off for him. He won the second of his three state titles. Even after Pieper moved out of the 119-pound

## NOT ALL ROADS LEAD TO GOLD

class, the weight was still loaded.

I went undefeated during the regular season and advanced to the state tournament for the fourth time. I won my first match at state and then advanced to face Bubolz in the state quarterfinals.

It was another close, hard-fought match and I earned a gritty 4-3 win in a battle of returning state champions. He took me down, but I battled back with a relentless attack and he was called twice for stalling.

I followed with an easy win in the semifinals before advancing to face Dennis Hall in the 1988 state finals. I was undefeated and looking to cap my high school career by winning a second straight Wisconsin state title.

Dennis was a junior and I was a senior. He had won state at 112 pounds as a freshman. At that point, he already was really well-known around the country in wrestling. He had done really well at Junior Nationals and was a standout in Greco-Roman wrestling.

You would've thought we had wrestled at some point before, but this would be our first meeting in competition.

I don't remember there being a ton of hype going into that match, but it was definitely a match people knew about and were anticipating.

Dennis and I were both state high school champions and we had both placed at Junior Nationals.

I had never wrestled him before, but I knew plenty about him. I had watched him compete and I obviously knew he was an excellent wrestler. But I hadn't felt and experienced what it was like to wrestle him in a match.

The whistle blew to start the match and I learned very quickly just how strong Dennis was. I was a guy who was typically the aggressor in my matches, but he wrestled a similar style where he put a lot of pressure on his opponents. We were both throwers. I also had a blast double-leg takedown and a fireman's carry that I could execute from my feet.

I could usually muscle people and overpower them. But I couldn't do that with Dennis Hall. The state finals match was

## A path of persistence, faith and perseverance

going to be a six-minute slugfest.

In the first two minutes, neither one of us could gain an advantage. It was 0-0 after the first period, but I had been warned for stalling. It was a call my coach thought was reasonable because I was wrestling tight. I chose neutral in the second period. For some reason, I didn't want to go down against him. I ended up scoring the match's only takedown in the second period. It was off an outside fireman's carry and I came out on top to earn a two-point takedown midway through second period. He was able to escape soon after that.

I was up 2-1 going into the third period and I was two minutes from capturing my second state championship.

Dennis chose down to start the third period and he quickly broke free for an escape. That deadlocked the match 2-2. It was going to come down to who could score a takedown. Or at least I thought it was.

Dennis was coming at me aggressively and I was warned for stalling. He was awarded a point to take a 3-2 lead. The earlier call made sense, but the second made no sense. We were both wrestling hard and the referee decided the match.

The greater frustration came being down 3-2, pressing him, and not earning a stall call. My coach was upset and I was upset. In hindsight, I should have chosen down in the second period. I also needed to be more offensive. I didn't make the necessary adjustments in the third period and it cost me the match.

At the same time, I remember being shocked that they called stalling on me at that juncture in the match. I had scored the only takedown of the match and had been wrestling aggressively.

I tried valiantly to score in the final seconds, but Dennis held me off. I lost the match 3-2. On a stalling call.

I scored the match's only takedown, and he scored on two escapes and a stalling call. The match should have gone into overtime, and my coach noted that "there were 10,000 fans, and 10,000 boos after the second stall call."

Time ran out and the match ended, I shook hands with Dennis, and he had his hand raised in the final match of my high

## NOT ALL ROADS LEAD TO GOLD

school career. I was stunned and devastated. A loss was not how I envisioned my high school career ending. Letting a referee determine the match's outcome made the loss more maddening.

I dejectedly walked off the main arena floor with my head down and my hands on my hips. I sat down in a hallway with my singlet straps pulled down. I was trying to comprehend what just happened. I didn't fully understand it at the time and it was a bitter pill to swallow. It was a rough way to end my high school career. It was awful.

A few minutes after I had sat down in the hallway, 1984 Olympic gold medalist Dave Schultz came up and started talking to me. He was an assistant coach at the University of Wisconsin.

Dave wanted to talk to me about possibly wrestling for the Badgers, but it obviously wasn't the ideal time for me after I had just suffered a heartbreaking loss in the state championship match.

I was very respectful to Dave, and he was someone I had great admiration for, but I said, "I'm sorry, I just can't do this right now." He understood and said, "Hey, no problem, I understand." He patted me on the back, and then turned around and walked away.

I don't like losing, especially the way I did in a match that meant so much. As the years went on, and I gained more experience, the losses stung just as bad or even more than they did when I was a kid.

There was enormous frustration associated with losing that match. I didn't push hard enough. I was also a little bit embarrassed because I lost on a stalling call in the state finals. It was a horrible way to lose in your biggest match of the season. I had a lot of people there to watch me. I felt like I had let them down.

My mindset was what it always was when I lost. I wanted another shot at him. I obviously had no idea at the time, but this was the start of a 15-year rivalry with Dennis Hall.

The state finals loss was a tough one to process. The assistant referee came up to me after the match and told me he

## A path of persistence, faith and perseverance

didn't agree with the stalling call. I know he was trying to be supportive, but it didn't help.

I couldn't forget what happened, but I had to move forward. I did what I typically did. I kept working. Nothing changed. I went through the same cycle in the spring and summer. I won the Greco and Freestyle state tournaments in Wisconsin again.

And then I headed to USA Wrestling's Junior Nationals at the UNI-Dome in Cedar Falls, Iowa. The brackets at Junior Nationals were massive. You would have 16 wrestlers in your bracket at the state high school tournament, but the brackets for Junior Nationals were insane.

I called my mom after weigh-ins for Junior Nationals and informed her there were more than 100 wrestlers in my bracket at 123 pounds. And there was one name that caught my attention: Dennis Hall. I was ready for another shot at the guy I had just suffered a heartbreaking state finals loss to a few months before.

The Junior Nationals Greco-Roman tournament started and it was quickly apparent that Dennis and I were on a collision course to meet in the finals. We were both rolling through the competition and we eventually landed spots in the national championship match. I was eager for another shot at him. And ready to avenge my loss from the state tournament.

I was looking for redemption, but I went out there and got hammered. This was Greco-Roman and I quickly discovered that Folkstyle wasn't Dennis Hall's best style of wrestling. It was Greco-Roman.

Dennis was light years ahead of me in Greco. I was down 8-0 before he pinned me. He was a significantly better thrower than I was in the body lock position. I never trained much in Greco back then, but I was strong with a good headlock and a good gut-wrench. Dennis was already training quite a bit in Greco and he was really proficient in that style.

He was very advanced for his age and it definitely showed. I felt like I showed up to a gun fight with a butter knife. He was the superior wrestler in that style.

I was more shell-shocked than anything. I had rolled past

## NOT ALL ROADS LEAD TO GOLD

everyone at Junior Nationals on my way to the finals. I figured I could avenge the loss to Dennis from state, but I had no idea he was that good in Greco. It was an eye-opener. I thought I was really good in Greco, but Dennis made me feel like a child.

I was 18 years old, and I remember thinking to myself, "Dang, I just got frickin' crushed by this guy." I had made the finals at Junior Nationals for the first time, but I had been beaten soundly by Dennis Hall in the finals. It was soul-crushing.

Even my own mother was surprised. Her comment to me was, "Why didn't you take first?" It hurt a little bit at first when my mom asked me why I didn't win the match. I had just finished second in a weight class with 109 wrestlers in it.

Knowing my mom, she didn't ask to hurt but to challenge. A congratulations would have been nice. My dad did what he always did. He told me, "I love you son and I am proud of you, and there are over 100 other wrestlers that would gladly trade places with you."

Those two matches against Dennis Hall in 1988 were just the beginning in what would become a long and epic rivalry that was mostly one-sided in his favor for over a decade.

After that loss in the finals at Junior Nationals, I was back in the weight room the following Monday trying to become stronger. And looking to improve after a tough setback. But knowing Dennis Hall, I am sure he was back training again as well.

The sting of another loss at the end of my high school career, especially to Dennis, drove me to become a better wrestler as I prepared to enter the collegiate ranks.

## CHAPTER 3
# BEN AND A BIBLE COLLEGE

While most of my classmates looked forward to graduation, I was content in high school. I was a successful athlete who was an 'A' or 'B' student while putting forth very little effort. I also worked 20-40 hours per week at a restaurant as a busboy/dishwasher/cook, so I figured I had enough money for most of my needs and wants.

I didn't have a clear path that I wanted to follow with my life. I knew I wanted to keep wrestling, but I needed to figure out how I could keep doing that. The future was uncertain mainly due to ignorance. I remember classmates talking about college, but college was something foreign to my family. My parents didn't go to college – they started working full-time right after finishing high school.

Despite all the unknowns and fears, I was drawing recruiting interest for wrestling from a few schools, but I wasn't 100 percent sure what I wanted to do. I graduated from high school, but still hadn't even applied to a college. It was July of 1988, and I needed to figure out my future plans.

There were two NCAA Division I schools that had been recruiting me. The University of Wisconsin in nearby Madison had shown interest. And Army, officially known as the United States Military Academy, had also expressed interest. St. Cloud State, an NCAA Division II school in Minnesota, also had recruited me. I

## NOT ALL ROADS LEAD TO GOLD

had drawn interest from those schools, but none of them offered me a scholarship for wrestling.

As an 18-year-old kid from a family with limited financial resources, I didn't have many options in terms of where I was going to attend college.

My parents thought it would be a good idea for me to go to college and encouraged me to pursue that route. My dad with visions that I would be a Division I wrestling stud in college, and my mom actually had a specific school in mind for me.

The school was Maranatha Baptist Bible College. The school was in Watertown, Wisconsin, a town of around 25,000 people located about midway between the state's largest cities of Milwaukee and Madison.

My mom encouraged me to go to Maranatha because our pastor said I should go there. My pastor, Mike Marshall, really wanted me to go to Maranatha – it was his alma mater.

Maranatha was a very small school of 450 students, but it had a big draw. Ben Peterson, a 1972 Olympic gold medalist who had wrestled alongside the legendary Dan Gable at Iowa State University, was the head coach at Maranatha.

A few years after Ben went to Iowa State and wrestled with Gable, he went to Maranatha to get his master's degree in theology and ended up staying there to coach wrestling and teach. He taught me in Introduction to Wrestling class and a Personal Evangelism class. Ben started at Maranatha in 1973, coached for a year and then resumed training for his silver medal performance at the 1976 Olympics. He then resumed coaching at Maranatha, where he stayed from 1976-2003. He coached there 28 years before retiring. He still lives in Watertown, Wisconsin.

Ben was interested in having me join his program and he drove down to my church and had a recruiting visit with me, my family, and my pastor. Ben asked me if I would like to join the wrestling program at Maranatha.

I knew a little bit about Ben because he spoke at my church during my sophomore year of high school. I met him during that time and he was aware of my credentials in wrestling. I liked Ben

## A path of persistence, faith and perseverance

and I made a visit to the campus at Maranatha.

Shortly after wrestling at Junior Nationals, I decided to go there. I applied to Maranatha just three weeks before the start of the fall semester. It was the only school that I visited.

Maranatha was a small private school that didn't offer athletic scholarships, but the school was relatively inexpensive. It cost between $6,000 and $10,000 a year over my five years there. I also qualified for a Pell Grant and the Wisconsin Tuition Grant that helped finance a large part of my college education. Unknown to me, my dad had also set aside some money for my brother and I which covered part of the first year. When I graduated from college, I was only $1,500 in debt, which obviously is an extremely low amount.

Maranatha was a near-perfect choice because I was immature as a young man and as a Christian. I needed limits and a strong person to enforce those limits. I didn't have a strong, consistent role model who lived and spoke what it was to be a biblical husband, father and neighbor – Ben Peterson became that person for me.

Ben was an icon in wrestling and even more as a Christian in wrestling. He became a father figure for me and filled a void in my life. Ben brought a unique approach to the sport of wrestling. And in the way he lived his life.

Ben is an individual who has this quiet intensity. He is a solid, grounded individual. We frequently butted heads when I was first started college. I was a goofy, aggressive kid and I said a lot of dumb and inappropriate things – wildly inappropriate for Maranatha. I was a Christian, but I was an immature Christian. I was going to this Baptist Bible college after being at a public high school. I wasn't used to being immersed in that system. It was a huge culture shock.

The fact that I didn't get kicked out of there is a testimony to the grace and patience of Maranatha and Ben Peterson. Mostly Ben.

Maranatha was incredibly strict in comparison to most private colleges, but especially compared to a secular institution.

## NOT ALL ROADS LEAD TO GOLD

You couldn't watch movies or videos, there was no TV in the rooms, and only approved music was allowed. You couldn't leave campus without permission.

You couldn't have facial hair at Maranatha. We had to wear a dress shirt, a tie, and slacks to class. If you went on a date, you had to have a chaperone. They had an approved chaperone list and you had to gain approval to do it. They had a rule where you couldn't be too close to a female. The students labeled it the "six-inch rule." You couldn't hold hands. If you did hold hands, someone in authority would see it and put a stop to it.

Initially, the dating rules didn't bother me. I didn't date at all in high school and the first three young ladies I asked out at Maranatha said no.

Maranatha was an ultra-conservative place. That is how they wanted to run their institution. And if you didn't abide by their rules, you would be sent home. Many of them were appropriate for 18- to 22-year-old students. They were trying to make sure the students made wise decisions. Kids are on their own for the first time in college and Maranatha provided a place where they removed all of the major distractions – drugs, sex, and alcohol (the internet and smart phones were years in the future). I wish they would have done it in a more graceful way. Philosophically, I believe that high school and college kids are adults in training. Rules are needed, but so is reasoning. Back then, they didn't provide much of an explanation for it. It's just the way it was.

When I first got there, I felt so out of place. If you lined everyone up and asked who didn't belong, it was me. I had no idea what the school was going to be like until I got up there. I didn't know what to expect culturally, socially, or academically. And I didn't know anybody when I got there.

Needless to say, Maranatha took me way out of my comfort zone. The one familiar aspect was that we could only use one version of the Bible – the King James version of the Bible. It was the same version used at my church.

To make matters worse, I got sick shortly after I started college. I had strep throat. Initially, I thought I had a bad sore throat. But after my neck swelled to where I couldn't button my shirt and swallowing water felt like swallowing crushed glass, I went to the emergency room. Within a week, the infection was gone but I developed an allergic reaction to the antibiotics and had my first experience with hives.

The first couple of weeks were miserable when I first arrived at Maranatha, but I never thought I was going to quit school. I had made a commitment to go to school there and I was going to honor it.

Eventually, life at Maranatha became better for me. I really enjoyed mathematics in high school and I decided early on I wanted to go into math education. Honestly, I didn't think too much about the decision. I was standing in line to determine my freshman class schedule, and one of the counselors asked what my major was.

"I don't know," was my initial response.

"What do you like?" the counselor asked.

"Math," I said.

"OK, you're Math Education," he said. "Here is the four-year plan."

It was one of the best unplanned decisions of my life. The math teacher at Maranatha was one of the greatest professors ever. His name was Dr. Curtis Malmanger, and I patterned much of what I would later do as a math teacher after him.

Dr. Malmanger also was an assistant football coach at the school. He was such a good professor. And he loved to talk sports. It was the perfect combination for me and we really hit it off.

Like most college students, I wasn't a fan of early morning classes. I had a Calculus class at 8 o'clock in the morning. I was falling asleep in class because I worked until 1 or 2 in the morning. I worked maintenance and security jobs on campus in the evenings to help pay for school.

After speaking with the Dr. Malmanger, Calculus 2 and 3 ended up being scheduled in the afternoon and I went from B in Calc 1 to A's in the higher Calcs.

My experience in the math department was great. I was

## NOT ALL ROADS LEAD TO GOLD

around a bunch of other math nerds. And there were a couple of girls who were studying math that were dating guys on the wrestling team and football team.

After the first couple of weeks of misery, I was fitting in and liking many aspects of school. I lived in a dormitory on campus, and between that, classes, and the wrestling team, I started gathering a decent friend group.

But some parts of Maranatha were still annoying. No movies meant no movie theaters or videos at home. And when you signed the Community Covenant, it also applied to all breaks, including summers.

During my junior year, I went out on a date with a young lady. Three couples drove. We drove an hour to the Milwaukee area, had dinner and stopped at my mom's place before we watched a movie. The young lady I was with felt guilty about it and turned us all in. I got called into the dean's office. They asked a bunch of questions and I admitted the misdeed and received a vast number of demerits. That's how strict they were at Maranatha. The place was very regimented, almost like the military.

On another occasion, one of my friends went out and got drunk and came back to the dorms. The school administrators found out about it. The next day, he was standing on the street with his suitcases packed and waiting for his parents to pick him up. He was kicked out of school.

Rules aside, my wrestling experience for Maranatha was a positive one. Maranatha competed in the NCCAA – notice the extra 'C' – the National Christian Collegiate Athletic Association.

It wasn't much of a transition from high school to the collegiate level I wrestled at. I went from being a three-time state finalist in high school to the equivalent of NCAA Division III or even lower in college. We competed mainly against smaller schools in the DII, DIII, Junior College and NAIA divisions.

I had a pretty successful freshman year in college. I placed in every tournament I was in and headed into my first national tournament wrestling well at 126 pounds.

I rolled to lopsided wins in my first two matches at my first

## *A path of persistence, faith and perseverance*

NCCAA tournament. I advanced to the finals against Kevin Byrd of Olivet Nazarene. He was a senior who had won the title the year before at 134 and was seeking his second national title.

Byrd was a good wrestler, but I was confident going into our finals match. I took control early and built a 12-0 lead before eventually winning by fall in under two minutes. I had captured my first NCCAA title.

It was my first national title in college, but it wasn't a shock to us that I won. People at other schools were surprised I beat him because Byrd was a returning national champ, a senior, and down a weight.

There were a few good wrestlers at the NCCAA level, but it wasn't exactly NCAA Division I either – although Charles Jones won two NCCAA titles for Olivet Nazarene, placed twice at the NAIA, and then won an NCAA title for Purdue.

There were guys wrestling in Division I that I had beaten in high school, but I wasn't looking to transfer anywhere.

During my freshman season, Ben Peterson came to me and asked if I was using Maranatha as a transition from high school to college wrestling. I told Ben I was going to stay at Maranatha. It was easily the second-best decision of my life. The first one was having a relationship with God through Christ. Staying at Maranatha kept me focused and kept me on track with my life. It was one of the most transformational decisions that led to qualifying the rest of my life. Maranatha was a distraction-free environment. And that's what I needed at that point in my life.

Ben Peterson was the person I needed at that point. He was the main reason I was successful. He was the example. He was there all the time. I watched him be a husband, watched him be a mentor and watched him be a coach. I saw how he was instilling his philosophies into me. I saw him and his wife, Jan, interact. I had a chance to see how they were as a couple. I also was around his brother, 1976 Olympic champion John Peterson, in the summers. John and his wife, Nancy, had a big impact on me as well.

The Petersons had strong values, and the love God and love

thy neighbor element. That was really important for me. My faith became stronger when I was in college. And the Peterson family helped me develop that.

Ben also understood wrestling at the highest level. He had won the Olympics and had reached the pinnacle in our sport. He had been the best wrestler in the world.

Ben understood immersing yourself into something while also being a man of faith. Ben and John Peterson weren't the greatest athletes, but they were successful because of the choices they made.

Ben was solid and consistent as a coach. He wasn't super dynamic – that's not Ben's personality. He's intense at moments, and he challenged me on so many occasions. He wasn't in your face, he had more of a quiet non-confrontational way of delivering his message when he thought it was appropriate.

When I won my first college match, I celebrated because it was exciting to win for the first time at that level. I had my hands up in the air and I ran around the mat.

A few minutes later, Ben quietly pulled me aside and said, "James, that's not how we act around here." He didn't embarrass me, but quietly got his message across. He would call me James when he wanted to get serious and make an important point with me.

The 'James' moments were not always bad, but they were always serious. One time I wasn't overly happy with Ben was when we were preparing to wrestle Loras College in a dual meet my junior year.

I was competing at 134 pounds and had just made weight for the dual meet. Right before the dual, Ben approached me in the locker room and said, "James, if you wrestle 158 pounds for us then we will have a chance to win the dual." No arguments, but I did say, "Man, Coach, why didn't you tell me that before I cut down to 134?"

I moved up three weight classes and beat the kid 7-2, but we lost the dual by five points. I didn't mind the challenge, but it would've been nice to have known I was going 158 before I cut

## A path of persistence, faith and perseverance

down to 134. I did have great respect for Ben – in every way. I just wasn't super happy with him that night.

From a technique point of view, Ben taught us the basics. He wrestled in the higher weight classes during his career. He was a bigger guy with a different body type than me, and his style of wrestling was completely different from mine. He showed us the meat and potatoes, the basic techniques, and let us develop our own style of wrestling.

His best techniques were a snatch single-leg and double-leg takedowns from his feet. He was a nasty leg rider from the top position where he could keep opponents down and turn them to their back. He also had an amazing roll which he insists he did not develop or name – the Peterson Roll. Other than the double, I did none of that and even my double was different from his.

I really evolved with my wrestling when I was in college. Ben provided the right environment through what he taught us and through allowing us to try and perfect what we were doing. I was always looking to improve my craft and my coach provided me with the environment to do that in.

During my sophomore season, Ben took me to the Midlands Championships to compete in 1989. Back then, the Midlands was considered the premier regular-season college tournament in the country and is still one of the toughest tournaments of the wrestling season. It had a storied history of top wrestlers who had competed there.

The Midlands featured the best NCAA Division I wrestlers and was held at Northwestern University in the Chicago suburb of Evanston, Illinois. It was just a short two-hour drive from our campus in Wisconsin. It was a tough two-day tournament that was held each year between Christmas and New Year's Day.

At that time, the Midlands also would attract top post-college wrestlers and aspiring Olympians who were allowed to compete.

The Midlands also provided an opportunity for top small college wrestlers like myself to occasionally sneak into and compete against the big boys from the larger colleges. My NCCAA Championship, which most D1 wrestlers would consider

## NOT ALL ROADS LEAD TO GOLD

being on par with a junior high state tournament, did not turn any heads.

Ben's reputation and relationship with Ken Kraft, the founder of the Midlands, is what solidified my appearance in the tournament. At that level, I was a nobody from a nothing wrestling college, but I was coached by Ben.

I had been challenged some my freshman year in college, but hardly at all the first part of my sophomore year. Ben knew I needed to be tested against better competition, so over Christmas break when the rest of the team was at home, I was entered into the Midlands Championships. Unbeknownst to me at the time, this was the beginning of a five-year wrestling crucible that provided all but a few of my most memorable and challenging college matches.

Ben Peterson meant so much to my career. What I did in my life doesn't happen without Ben Peterson. He was one of those people who was put in your life by God to enable you to maximize who you can be.

Ben always seemed to know what was best for me and he played a monumental role in my development as an athlete. He pointed and I went – and he was pointing at the Midlands.

When the pairings came out, I wasn't seeded and was drawn into the bracket, which hadn't happened in a long time. At this point, I knew I would face a challenging road. But this was where Ben wanted me to be. And it was an opportunity to wrestle some of the best college guys in the country.

I won my first match by fall over West Virginia's Scott Blair and then expected to battle No. 3 seed Shawn Charles of Arizona State in the second round.

But Charles, who went on to become a four-time All-American and two-time NCAA finalist, was upset by unseeded Craig Campbell of Eastern Illinois in the first round. Campbell was a quality opponent, but I took command early en route to earning a methodical 4-1 victory.

I followed by earning a close, hard-fought win over Bucknell's Chris Doukas in the quarterfinals. The match ended in

## A path of persistence, faith and perseverance

a 2-2 deadlock and I won by criteria – my takedown beat his two escapes.

I had won my first three matches at the Midlands, defeating three Division I opponents from larger schools to reach the semifinal round. I didn't fully appreciate what occurred. But at the time, I was ignorant and a bit naïve of the larger college wrestling world and went to the Midlands with the same confidence I had in most matches.

I'm sure the guys I was wrestling didn't even know where Maranatha was. My guess is that they most likely overlooked a non-DI wrestler like myself. Looking back now, I realize the gravity of what happened.

I knew I could compete with the guys from the bigger schools, and those victories were confirmation that I was more than capable of holding my own against wrestlers from college's highest level.

But this was the semifinals of the Midlands, and I ran into a strong opponent. I battled No. 2 seed Doug Wyland of North Carolina, and suffered a 12-6 setback in the semifinals. Doug went on to finish second, losing to Jack Cuvo 3-2 in the finals. Wyland placed fourth at the NCAA Division I tournament that season.

The match I lost was a good lesson for me and proved I still had plenty to work on. I came back to win in the consolation semifinals, powering to a 12-2 major decision over Missouri's Buddy Smith. I had advanced to the third-place match at the Midlands. And clinched a top-four finish in a 126-pound weight class that had 33 entries.

I drew another tough wrestler in the third-place match and came up short. I suffered a 5-1 setback to No. 5 seed Adam DiSabato of Ohio State. Adam placed sixth at the NCAA Championships later that season.

The Midlands Championships was an important experience for me. I had placed fourth in my first appearance at the Midlands as an unseeded wrestler from a tiny Bible college in Wisconsin. But I was far from content with how I finished.

I was wrestling these top guys from these massive Division I

## NOT ALL ROADS LEAD TO GOLD

schools and I was from this little tiny religious school. But I also was used to winning so I wasn't happy about the matches that I lost.

Evaluating my performance, I wasn't cutting a lot of weight and I felt strong at 126 – a lesson learned in high school. When you wrestle a lot of matches in a big tournament, and are not cutting hard, you don't have to fight through the emptiness of a deep cut. Wyland was the only one that felt as strong, even though his technique was better – but that could be fixed. My conditioning level was high – and that paid off for me.

The Midlands was a big deal and it was a huge tournament, but it wasn't overwhelming. Ben felt like I belonged there and he had me believing I did, too.

I had wrestled in big national tournaments before when I competed at the Cadet and Junior Nationals. And I had wrestled some of the best guys in the country in freestyle and Greco-Roman during the summer months.

I had trained with bigger guys in the practice room before the Midlands and that really helped me when I competed against guys at 126 who were my size. Placing fourth at the Midlands, it really legitimized what I could do.

I always learned from my losses. I was never happy about losing. It always stung – even when I lost to someone who was better than me. The longer I wrestled, the greater the pain was from losing.

At the same time, I was earning my share of praise for placing fourth in a tournament of that caliber. My ego inflated and I didn't learn the greater lesson from the Midlands until it was too late.

When I returned to my own level of wrestling at the collegiate level, the competition was subpar in comparison. I wasn't as focused as I should have been in the second half of my sophomore season. And it cost me. I entered my second NCCAA tournament as a sophomore and dominated the competition as expected. I rolled into the finals again and figured I would just power my way to my second national title.

Why not? He was from same school that I had crushed the

## *A path of persistence, faith and perseverance*

year before in the finals. There was no one good at my weight in the NCCAA. Yet here I was in a fight against Gabriel Mendez of Olivet Nazarene University that I wasn't ready for.

He was ready for me. I tried to go upper body and he attacked my legs. He picked me apart. He was a little bit faster and slicker than me. I didn't expect a tough opponent like that and I lost. It wasn't even close. I lost 14-7 in the finals of our national tournament.

After the match, I learned that Mendez was from Mexico. He was a bronze medalist at the 1986 Pan American Championships. He was a more mature wrestler that was prepared. The missed lesson from the Midlands was learned in hindsight – overlook no one.

It was embarrassing. I was stunned. I was upset. It was a huge blow to my ego. I had rolled through this tournament the year before and I had placed fourth at Midlands during my sophomore season. But then I lost in the Christian national finals. It was a tough and unexpected loss that I didn't see coming.

I had grown arrogant, and the loss knocked me down a few pegs. In hindsight, it was a valuable lesson I needed to help me regain humility and teach me to underestimate no one.

I remember getting back home from that tournament. I got off the bus, put my bags down in the locker room and went right into the weight room to work out. I was mad and my response to setbacks was always to get stronger. Being stronger makes things easier. I always believed that. There is always an answer.

Working out after we arrived home was a good way for me to blow off steam. Lifting weights was better than grabbing a kid by the throat and choking him.

For the most part, I learned my lessons whenever I lost a match. I had an ability to use the setbacks as motivation to help me come back stronger. I came back my junior year at Maranatha and had another successful season. I bumped up a weight class to 134 pounds. That wasn't a problem for any tournament except the Midlands. I wasn't overlooked this time and was seeded sixth.

The one weight class jump, and the addition of the storied

## NOT ALL ROADS LEAD TO GOLD

University of Iowa program, saw my worst performance at the Midlands. I won the first two matches, but then ran into No. 3 seed Mark Marinelli from Ohio State. He crushed me 13-1. Mark went on to place fourth at the NCAA Championships that season.

I dropped down to the consolation quarters and ran into my brother, Alan, who normally wrestled 142 but decided to drop to 134 for the Midlands. My brother forfeited to me which I didn't completely understand because he seemed to enjoy beating me in most of our practice matches.

In the next match, I lost to an Iowa backup and fell just short of placing in the top six. I finished in the top eight. I went 3-2 and was one win away from reaching the medal podium again after moving up a weight class.

The next two years were pretty much rinse and repeat. I went on to win NCCAA titles my junior and senior seasons to finish as a three-time National Christian College Athletic Association Champion.

My second year at 134 saw a significant improvement in my Midlands performance. Despite the eventual top three finishers in the NCAA Championships populating the bracket, I came back strong at the Midlands to take third as a senior in college in 1991.

After plowing through my first two opponents from Missouri and Lehigh, I received one of the toughest and best lessons of my wrestling life in the quarterfinals of the 1991 Midlands Championships.

I stepped onto the mat to face Iowa's Tom Brands, who would win three NCAA titles before capturing Olympic and World titles for the United States.

I always thought I was strong until I squared off against Tom Brands at the Midlands. He broadened my definition of strong to include relentless.

I held my own in the first period. He was strong, and I was strong. He was physical, and I was physical. I made a small position mistake and Brands scored a takedown. I followed with an escape at the end of the period. I only trailed 2-1 after the first period, but his hard-nosed approach was already taking its toll on

## A path of persistence, faith and perseverance

me.

The intensity level he wrestled at was phenomenal. Midway through the second period, I was struggling to match his level of wrestling. His pressure was superhuman and the longer the match went the greater the gap.

He continued to attack with his relentless style and led 7-3 in the second period before he eventually beat me by a final score of 15-5. The third period, Brands scored two takedowns and four stalling points. A 10-second scramble to avoid a takedown at the end of the match nearly broke me. If the match had lasted another 30 seconds, my heart may have exploded.

I had never wrestled anybody who could match my strength and maintain that kind of pressure. Tom Brands basically pulled my lungs out of my body and was stepping on them because he was in such tremendous physical condition. He was relentless in a way I had never felt before. Tom was next level with his wrestling. He had muscular endurance that was off the charts. He was breathing hard, but he still kept his foot on the gas pedal and mashed it to the floor the whole match. It was impressive. He never let up until the final whistle blew.

It was one of the most transformative moments of my wrestling career. The beating I took from Tom Brands prepared me for wrestling Dennis Hall in later years at the international level. That high physicality and pressure that Hall competed with was the same style that Brands wrestled with. When you encounter a quality that is overwhelming, there is a choice to run from it or to replicate it. I walked off the mat after wrestling Brands thinking I am never going to get beat again because of conditioning – especially muscular endurance which is the cornerstone of relentlessness. That experience drove my training. I wanted that next level muscular endurance the Brands brothers had.

Following the Brands beatdown, I rattled off four close wins – 7-3 over Scott Hassel of Northern Iowa, 5-4 over Jody Jackson of Virginia, 3-2 over Dan Carcelli of Cleveland State and 6-5 over Ray Serbick of Eastern Illinois for third. My quarterfinal consolation match was a rematch against Hassell, who had

## NOT ALL ROADS LEAD TO GOLD

defeated me 1-0 at the Northern Open. Even though I had been dismantled by Brands, I came back strong and I was trending in the right direction.

I continued to excel in the Midlands while competing there after my college eligibility had finished. I was third at the Midlands in 1992 and fourth in 1993.

In 1992, I won my first three matches before running into North Carolina's T.J. Jaworsky in the semifinals. Jaworsky, who went on to win three NCAA titles, beat me 7-2 in the semis.

T.J. was really good – he was a stud. I was half a step behind him in terms of speed and technique. I don't remember him overpowering me. He was a good technical wrestler who seemed like he was never out of position.

In the 1993 Midlands, I met Jaworsky again in the semifinals and he pinned me. I was shell-shocked because I had never been pinned in college. Despite placing third the year before, I came in as the No. 5 seed because three NCAA champs were in the weight.

What was even more frustrating is that I had moved to Colorado Springs in November to start my Greco career and was finally wrestling high level athletes every day. I dominated my first three opponents and thought I would fare better against Jaworsky. I don't even remember how I was pinned. Jaworsky lost to Cary Kolat, who went on to win multiple World medals for the U.S., in the Midlands finals that year. I lost to Tony Purler, a 1993 NCAA champion.

Those Midlands matches were instrumental for me and would serve me well during the next phase of my wrestling career.

Competing in the Midlands was a huge bonus for me during my time at Maranatha. It enabled me to measure myself against some of the very best guys in the country. Many of whom would go on to be the best in the World.

In addition to Ben and his direction, having my brother, Alan, wrestle with me in college made a huge difference for me. He was a great training partner and it obviously was nice having my brother there at college with me. Maranatha didn't have a D1 wrestling environment that automatically elevated your toughness

## A path of persistence, faith and perseverance

and intensity, but having Ben Peterson as a coach and a brother who was an amazing athlete provided a similar opportunity for growth.

Al was an excellent athlete who was bigger and faster and stronger than me. I'm 5-foot-4 and he's 5-7. He started playing football as a junior in college and ended up being pretty good. He is decent at basketball, and he is an excellent golfer. Al was a gifted athlete who was really good at whatever he threw himself into.

What he threw himself into most was beating me. You wouldn't know it by our competition results, but spend any time watching the two of us train and the picture became all too clear. Al was the better wrestler. What also became clear was the only thing athletically that I was better at than Al was competing.

My brother was a two-time state finalist in high school who won the National Christian Collegiate Athletic Association title four times for Maranatha. He was a weight class above me. I wrestled 126 and 134 during my college career. Al came in at 134 and moved up to 142. We were our main training partners – it was definitely the case of iron sharpens iron.

The same recipe for success we had enjoyed in high school was revisited in college and enhanced by Ben Peterson. Fierce brotherly competition. We hammered each other in that wrestling room. He was a beast in practice. I don't remember beating him that often in practice, especially in our upperclassman years. I do remember one practice when he took me down six times and then stopped. I insisted we continue. He disagreed and I punched him.

Our wrestling matches resembled mixed martial arts, where we essentially were fighting each other. When we fought, Ben would separate us but not right away. With several brothers of his own, and one who trained with him for over a decade, Ben appreciated a good brother scrap. But this was Maranatha and fights were frowned upon.

In college, my brother and I fought much less than high school, but there was the occasional explosion. We also had a deep love for each other. Any time anyone beat Al, I made it a point to destroy their teammate. We developed a strong bond in college. I

## NOT ALL ROADS LEAD TO GOLD

never got the sense that Al enjoyed competing as much as I did, but in one match everything I knew my brother could be as a wrestler became a reality. The only downside was that it took me losing for Al to get there.

After I lost in the national finals in college as a sophomore at 126 pounds, my brother had a kid from the same school in the next finals match at 134. I've rarely seen a guy beat a man that bad. He unleashed the Dobermans on that guy – it was awesome. I know it definitely made me feel better. He did nothing illegal, but the opposing coaches had to carry his opponent back to their bench.

Al was highly successful in college and he had a chance to keep wrestling after college. The USA National coaches talked to him about wrestling Greco-Roman after college, but he decided he was done. He walked away from wrestling and did not look back after college. He was done with the pressure of competing.

Even after I started training internationally, I would come back home and wrestle with him. And he would still beat me. That's how good my brother was.

There is no chance my college wrestling would have been elevated to the level of placing at the Midlands without Al. His desire to beat me pushed and drove me to higher levels of excellence.

It was instrumental having my brother there with me for the first two-plus decades of my life. God puts different people in your life for different reasons. If it weren't for my brother battling me every single day, we would not have been the wrestlers we ended up being. We drove each other relentlessly. He provided that physical and emotional challenge that helped my development.

I finished my collegiate career at Maranatha with a 141-16 record. All but two of the losses were to Division I athletes. I won three NCCAA titles while being named Outstanding Wrestler of the tournament in 1989 and 1991. I also placed third twice and fourth twice at the Midlands Championships, the most prestigious college event aside from NCAAs. By my fifth year, I was in the Midlands 20-win club with 22 wins.

My wrestling improved and I also became a better student.

*A path of persistence, faith and perseverance*

My grades in college were a bit better than high school and I finished with a 3.4 grade-point average. School came easily for me, but I didn't apply myself. However, after years of being badgered by my mother, I finally did push hard enough and was able to earn straight A's in college my last three semesters.

I graduated from Maranatha with a bachelor's degree in Secondary Math Education. That degree would serve me well as I continued to chase my goals and dreams in wrestling at the next level. But I wasn't completely sure I was going to keep wrestling.

When I was finishing my degree in the spring of 1993. I called my mom. I told her I was making a decision. "I'm going to stop wrestling and start teaching," I said matter-of-factly.

I had thought I was done, and I didn't have a clear road. The same uncertainty and fear of the unknown after high school was now plaguing me as I was finishing college. My mom wasn't so sure I should stop competing.

"I remember when you were in high school and you said your goal was to be an Olympic champion," she said. "If you stop, you will have never tried and you will never know. I don't think God would want you to stop wrestling."

My mother's words stopped me in my tracks. She challenged me. Who knows what direction my life would've gone if she hadn't said that? I wasn't sure where to go with my life and my mom stepped in and gave me direction. I needed to keep wrestling. She was right and I thank God that she wasn't afraid to speak her mind to me at a time when I really needed to hear those words.

I called U.S. National Greco-Roman Coach Mike Houck to see what I needed to do to continue wrestling. Mike was the first American to become a World champion (1985) in Greco-Roman and was now leading the U.S. program in that classic style of wrestling.

Mike had also wrestled for Ben Peterson at Maranatha College, and had assisted Ben my freshman year. He also helped train me a bit in Greco-Roman wrestling before he moved on after graduating. I talked to Mike and he told me to enter three tournaments in Greco-Roman.

# NOT ALL ROADS LEAD TO GOLD

I wrestled in April's U.S. Senior Nationals in Las Vegas and fell one win short of placing in the top eight. But I came back strong at University Nationals and the Olympic Festival to catch Mike's attention. I placed third at the 1993 University Nationals in Greco before I won the U.S. Olympic Festival.

Mike was looking for wrestlers to join the inaugural Greco-Roman resident-athlete program at the United States Olympic Training Center in Colorado Springs.

After I placed in those two events, Mike picked me to come to the OTC and train in Greco. I was one of 16 wrestlers accepted into the inaugural resident program for Greco-Roman. I had found my way again.

Once I qualified for the resident-athlete program at the Olympic Training Center, I knew the Olympics were a more realistic goal for me. I was going to have the training partners and the coaches to help me get there.

The first time I wrestled at the U.S. Senior Nationals in Greco-Roman I learned a hard lesson. I wrestled Buddy Lee in my first match. He was the No. 1 guy and I hit him with a headlock early in the match and took a 3-0 lead. I was feeling pretty good for a few seconds, but he came right back and smashed me.

Buddy was a seasoned Greco guy who excelled on the international level. And he took it to me. The final score was 14-3. I learned that I sucked from the down position, known as par terre, and had been exposed at the Senior level. Buddy Lee turned me like a top and twisted me into a pretzel. I had no answer. I couldn't stop him.

That setback to Lee was a huge reality check and a big wake-up call for me. I definitely realized if I was going to do something at this level I needed to improve considerably. My confidence had been shaken and was one of the reasons I thought I might be done wrestling.

Having been accepted into the United States Greco-Roman program provided me with a renewed confidence. And now there was work to do.

## CHAPTER 4
# ROCKY MOUNTAIN HIGH

It was an exciting time for the United States Greco-Roman program. The new Olympic Training Center resident-athlete program was about to be launched. And I was one of the 16 members in the inaugural class.

I was pumped up about heading to Colorado Springs to live and train at the OTC. I put everything I owned into my used Toyota Tercel and headed west for the Rocky Mountains of Colorado on November 1, 1993.

The downside was I had no job and no money. My parents had no way to support my Olympic aspirations, but I was determined to make my new arrangement work. The upside, as a resident-athlete, was that my food and housing were taken care of by USA Wrestling. I was provided three meals a day in the Olympic Training Center cafeteria and I lived in the dormitories on the OTC complex.

I also had a roommate, another aspiring young Olympic-caliber wrestler named Broderick Lee. Broderick was super respectful and we developed a good relationship during the three years we roomed together. He wrestled in the weight class below me and we trained together frequently.

Broderick was a gifted athlete and someone I remembered from my Junior National Greco days. He was a dynamic thrower and I recall him and Dennis having a good match my junior summer in high school. Broderick and Dennis competed a weight

## NOT ALL ROADS LEAD TO GOLD

class above me at 123 pounds. Broderick won three NCAA Division II titles for Portland State and was an excellent collegiate wrestler. He was an explosive and talented wrestler who was a tough matchup for anyone he faced. And he was a great training partner. He made one World Team in 1997 and then faded from the Greco scene by 2001.

Unfortunately, Broderick battled some demons off the mat. He had some personal issues and he ended up in a bad place in his life. In 2003, a few years after he finished competing, he died of an apparent suicide. It crushed me when it happened. It was shocking news when I heard about it. It was totally unexpected.

I knew Broderick had a daughter who he loved dearly. I didn't see the suicide coming at all. I wish I could've done something to help him. It was obviously a bad deal. I recall the moment I heard the news of his death – I was sitting in my office and just began sobbing. I had positive memories of the time that Broderick and I roomed together. We had grown close in our three years together at the OTC. It was heartbreaking when I heard what had happened to Broderick. He had certainly done a great deal to help me during my first few years in Colorado.

Living and training at the Olympic Training Center was the ideal situation for a young wrestler like me who was just out of college.

Having your food and housing paid for was an awesome benefit for the wrestlers. But I also needed to find a job to help offset my other expenses – gas, insurance, entertainment and college loans. Shortly after I arrived at the OTC, I was fortunate to be able to find a job. There was a young lady I knew who had been a cheerleader at Maranatha, and she was married and living in Colorado Springs.

She found out that I was accepted to the OTC as a resident-athlete. She remembered I was a math major and we were friends in college. She was working at a Christian school – Hilltop Baptist High School – in the Springs. She mentioned to the principal that I was coming out there and had a math background. They brought me in for an interview and I ended up teaching

## A path of persistence, faith and perseverance

there for the next 12 years. They were desperate for a math teacher, having gone through three by November, and I was desperate for a math job.

My first week in Colorado, I landed a teaching job. I was going to teach five classes a day, but I had to negotiate with the principal so I could still make the morning and afternoon practices at the Olympic Training Center.

I taught five classes a day, the same schedule a full-time teacher would have. But I wasn't there the entire day, so I was considered part-time. I taught five classes, but they only paid me $6,000 a year when I started at Hilltop Baptist High School in 1993. It wasn't much money, especially for all of the work I was doing, but it was a job. Plus, the school was flexible in making sure I had time to make it to wrestling practices and competitions.

The money I did make was enough for me to live on with my room and board already taken care of at the OTC. And it was the best way for me to pursue my dream of becoming an Olympic champion. It was not an easy road, working that hard for a very small amount of money.

Teaching math was something I enjoyed. I loved math. I had a busy schedule with very few breaks. I taught algebra, geometry, trigonometry, consumer math and calculus.

To say my daily schedule was chaotic would be a massive understatement. My days were long and jam-packed with wrestling workouts sandwiched around a full day of teaching. I would wake up each morning at 7:30, eat a banana and then head into the OTC wrestling room for the morning technique session or strength training. Practice would end and I would shower before hustling over to the cafeteria to eat breakfast. I also packed a lunch from the OTC that I could eat while I was at school.

I would then jump in my car and drive to the high school. I would teach five classes straight through from 10:30 a.m. to 3:30 p.m. When my last class of the day ended, I drove back to the OTC for our tougher practice of the day from 4 p.m. to 6:30 p.m.

The afternoon practices featured a bigger emphasis on live

## NOT ALL ROADS LEAD TO GOLD

wrestling. They were grueling as I trained with some of the best athletes in the country.

Following practice, I would eat dinner with my teammates in the OTC cafeteria. By the time I finally got back to my dorm room, I was exhausted. It's a good thing that I was still relatively young and still had an abundance of energy. My schedule was challenging, grueling and draining. I was training full-time and basically teaching full-time. I definitely had to be disciplined with everything I did.

When I came to the Olympic Training Center, it also was a significant transition for me. It was the first time I had been away from Maranatha, which was super strict. Coming to Colorado Springs was a real test of my faith because I was now really on my own for the first time in my life. I had the freedom to do whatever I wanted. I didn't have people looking over my shoulder so I could make the right moral decisions. It was the first time I really had to make my faith my own.

Luckily, I taught in an environment that helped me in that respect. The school I worked at also was in the same building as the church I attended. I went to Hilltop Baptist Church, which was affiliated with my school.

Fortunately, I was really focused on my goals and I was making wise choices. My wrestling also improved considerably once I started training in the highly competitive practice room at the OTC. Everybody in that room was good. You had to meet certain requirements to train there, so the quality of practice partners was top-notch.

If you tried to coast in practice, you would be exposed. That was why the resident-athlete program was so beneficial. It brought the best guys in the country together to train in one location. It was definitely a case of iron sharpens iron as we trained against the nation's elite.

The first couple of months felt like a roundhouse kick to the brain box. The athletes in the new Greco resident-athlete program had already been training for a month. They were immersed in their training. I arrived a month late so I could finish my student

## *A path of persistence, faith and perseverance*

teaching and finish my degree.

I was new and from the smallest college, and my only connection was the coach. These guys already had a month of forming relationships. The last thing I needed was to get labeled as someone who "didn't belong." I charged forward in the training without even considering the physical impact.

What stands out the most from that first week of training were the medicine ball sit-ups. I had never done medicine ball sit-ups, let alone with a 16-pound ball being thrown at you on a decline bench. I did every rep and every set for the next week. It took such a toll that I couldn't sit up because of the stabbing pain in my abs. I had to roll to my stomach and put my legs over the mattress to get out of bed. I could not sit up. I had to grab the back of my legs for sit-ups in practice and each one was excruciating.

Playing catch-up sucks. I was behind in the physical fitness, I was working a full-time job, and my Greco skills were subpar. I was getting the crap kicked out of me daily, especially after the missed month. Fortunately, the team was welcoming and my faith saw me through the worst moments.

The daily abuse eased as I learned to train at the Olympic level. My body rose to the occasion and my skills improved to the point where I could start handing out some pain rather than being just a recipient.

My progression became apparent when I entered the 1994 U.S. Nationals in Las Vegas at 62 kilograms/136.5 pounds. The Sunkist Kids, one of the nation's top wrestling clubs, was interested in possibly adding me to their roster of Greco-Roman athletes. The Sunkist Kids paid for my hotel room in Las Vegas. They also told me that if I placed in the top six at my weight class that I could join their club.

I had a strong tournament and I placed fourth at the U.S. Nationals. That landed me a spot in the Sunkist Kids, which was the nation's premier club for Greco at that time. Earning a spot with the Sunkist Kids was huge for me. Clubs like Sunkist, the New York Athletic Club and the Minnesota Storm would sponsor aspiring Olympic athletes with financial backing.

## NOT ALL ROADS LEAD TO GOLD

Once I joined the Sunkist Kids, they would help pay for my trips by taking care of my flight and hotel while also giving me a per diem for meals. Having that sponsorship for Sunkist was saving me a lot of money and allowing me to travel to tournaments I needed to compete in. Having them take care of my travel expenses was really important for me so I could gain experience against top-level competition. Sunkist probably spent anywhere from $6,000 to $8,000 a year on me so I could travel to events. That was a relief and a huge boost for me. There is no way I could have afforded to compete in all of those tournaments without their assistance.

Following the U.S. Nationals, my new sponsor paid for me to travel to northern California to compete in the Concord Cup. It was a top Greco-Roman event that featured top domestic and foreign competitors.

The event opened my eyes to the Greco landscape at 62 kg. The three guys who had placed above me at the 1994 Nationals either dropped out of the event or didn't place. One of them took the meal per diem and didn't even enter the tournament.

The 1994 Concord Cup also marked the resumption of my rivalry with Dennis Hall although it wasn't much of a rivalry back then. Dennis had beaten me twice in 1988 – in the Wisconsin state high school finals and in the Junior Nationals Greco-Roman finals.

Dennis was competing at a weight class below me at the time, but he moved up a division when he competed at the Concord Cup. It had been nearly six years since we had wrestled, but I was still thinking redemption after losing to Dennis earlier. But it wasn't much of a match. I wasn't even a speed bump for him. He stomped me by a score of 14-3. I scored early in the match against Dennis, but then he took it to me. He body-locked me, he gut-wrenched me. He tossed me all over the mat. He had moved up a weight class for that event, but it didn't seem to faze him. I did manage to place fourth despite being dominated by Hall.

Dennis Hall showed just how good he was that season. He

## A path of persistence, faith and perseverance

went on to win a World bronze medal for the United States later that year at the World Championships.

I followed the Concord Cup by placing third at the U.S. World Team Trials. That put me on the U.S. National Team at 62 kg. The top three wrestlers in each weight class made the National Team. I went from being unranked in the country to being on the National Team. That was a big jump for me. During that time, U.S. National Team members received monthly stipends of $900, $500 and $300 for the top three guys. I started making around $300 per month as the No. 3 guy on the ladder. It wasn't much, but it definitely helped. And that was incentive to want to move up the ladder and make more money.

Just as my wrestling career had finally started improving, my personal life decided it wanted to punch me in the face. I was engaged to a young lady and it was only three weeks before we were supposed to get married. I had just won the Olympic Festival, and when I returned home to Colorado, I was excited to share the news with her about my experience. But she didn't want to hear any more about my wrestling career. I started talking to her about winning the tournament, but then she jumped in with a comment of her own.

"I think you love wrestling more than you love me," she said matter-of-factly. "You have to make a choice between me and wrestling."

The news was stunning, to say the least. Talk about having the rug pulled out from under you. I had no idea whatsoever that was coming. I had no inkling. I was excited about becoming married and then this happened. I felt like I got punched in the gut – and I didn't see the fist coming. I was blindsided.

It wasn't exactly what I expected to come home to, but I also believe everything happens for a reason. I was just in shock. It was a little bit of a blur. How do you process something like that? I think her perception was wrong, and I knew God wanted me to wrestle. She asked me to make a choice between her and wrestling, but it was really a decision between her and God.

## NOT ALL ROADS LEAD TO GOLD

We had been dating two years and had been engaged for a year and a half. I asked her to give me the engagement ring back, and she sent it back to me. I was an emotional mess. It was the summer of 1994 and it was a rough time. My wrestling was inconsistent for the next year – it was a struggle for me to get back on track.

The following season, I placed fifth at the 1995 U.S. Nationals. It was a step back for me after I had been ranked No. 3 in the country. Obviously, I didn't wrestle as well. I lost to Shon Lewis in the semifinals and then lost my next match before taking fifth. It wasn't a good performance.

Following Nationals, the Concord Cup was a perfect example of my erratic wrestling. I stepped on the mat to face two-time World champion and Olympic silver medalist Rifat Yildiz of Germany in Concord.

I came out and took it to him. I beat Yildiz by technical superiority in a match that lasted just three minutes after I built a 10-point advantage to end it. I hit him in a headlock and then I lifted him with a gut wrench. He was wrestling up a weight class, but it was still a signature win for me to beat a wrestler of his caliber. You turn some heads when you crush a multiple medalist. It was an important victory for me because I had been struggling earlier in that season. I struggled in my next two matches before finishing third.

Despite my roller coaster performance at Concord, I still had to prepare for the 1995 World Team Trials, but disaster struck a week before the competition. I was playing soccer in an indoor league to cross train in between wrestling workouts when a freak accident occurred.

There was a free ball in the middle of the field and I was hustling over to kick it. A player from the opposing team also was sprinting toward the ball. We arrived simultaneously and we went to kick the ball at the same time. His foot was bigger than mine and I paid the price. My ankle popped in one place and then I stepped and it popped in another.

I had broken my right ankle. It swelled up like a watermelon

## A path of persistence, faith and perseverance

and turned black and blue. Not only was the ankle broken, but I had managed to sprain my entire ankle. The break was technically called an avulsion fracture. One of my ligaments pulled a piece of bone off my ankle. It was a gruesome injury. And the timing couldn't have been much worse. I was in horrible pain and I was going to miss the biggest event of the season because I was injured playing another sport. Such a stupid move.

U.S. Assistant National Coach Anatoly Petrosyan, who grew up in the Soviet Union, was pissed.

"Jim, why you play soccer?" Anatoly said in broken English while shaking his head in frustration. "Jim, when you were boy, you listen to your mother and father?"

"Yes," I responded.

"Well, now I'm your mother and father," Anatoly said sternly. "And you listen to me, no soccer."

He was right and I knew it. Playing soccer was a stupid move. A week later, and still barely able to walk, I was not able to wrestle at the World Team Trials. I lost my spot on the National Team and I lost the money I received from being ranked in the top three in my weight class.

I also became aware that the club who sponsored me, the Sunkist Kids, was not super happy with me. I think they were talking about not sponsoring me anymore. Instead of them calling me to book my flights and hotels, I would have to call them and ask to go to tournaments. They agreed to send me, but I had to prove myself all over again. Did I mention how dumb it is to play soccer the week before the World Team Trials?

Being an Olympic-level athlete, the results speak for themselves. If you excel and produce, you will be taken care of. It you don't, you won't last long. Wrestling, like most sports at the highest level, is a results-driven endeavor.

Overall, my results were decent, even inconsistent means there is some good. There was light at the end of the tunnel. After a year of not dating, I met my future wife. It was the summer of 1995 and I was working a camp with my college coach, Ben Peterson, at Camp Forest Springs. The camp was in northern

## NOT ALL ROADS LEAD TO GOLD

Wisconsin. We ran summer wrestling camps up there. It was held in a beautiful location and situated right on a lake.

One day at the camp, I was looking for a phone book because I wanted to go see a movie. I asked a receptionist at the camp if she had one. The young lady, Rachel Holtum, couldn't find a phone book and I kind of teased her about it. She was an English major and we started talking. I challenged her to a game of Scrabble and I crushed her.

She said she would never date a wrestler, but I was determined to change that after we met. After the camp, I went back to Colorado Springs. Rachel was teaching violin classes in Ames, Iowa. We wrote letters to each other three times a week and called each other once a week. She came out to Colorado to visit me.

On our first date, we went to watch one of my Greco-Roman wrestling teammates, Matt Lindland, in a Tough Guy fight. It wasn't a good call on my part. Rachel's father is a librarian and she's a musician. Being around combat sports wasn't her world. It wasn't a good choice for me to bring her into the high testosterone world that I was immersed in.

The wiser move was taking her sightseeing on her trip to Colorado. We went and explored the majestic Garden of the Gods Park and I showed her around Colorado Springs. It's a beautiful and scenic city with majestic, snow-capped Pikes Peak towering over it.

During the Christmas holiday, I visited my family in Wisconsin and then visited Rachel's family in Iowa City, Iowa. Her dad was a librarian at the University of Iowa. Living in the wrestling mecca of Iowa City, Rachel was aware of the tradition of excellent college wrestling with the Iowa Hawkeyes. She had her picture taken with Iowa coach and wrestling legend Dan Gable when she was 11 years old.

Rachel and I lived apart for the first year after we started dating. In June of 1996, I was ready to take the next step in our relationship. After a year of being in a long-distance relationship, I proposed to her and she accepted. She landed a job teaching at

## *A path of persistence, faith and perseverance*

the same school I worked at. Rachel moved to Colorado in August and she rented an apartment in the Springs.

Knowing the craziness of summer camps and tournaments, we planned a wedding for the only free time we both had during spring break. I was returning from a tournament in Russia and flew back into Denver. Ethan Bosch and Chris Mirabella picked me up from the airport and we drove to Freeport, Illinois for the wedding. Rachel's mother grew up in Freeport, and most of her family was still living there. We were married on March 8, 1997, in Freeport.

We spent a short, three-day honeymoon at Disney World's Epcot Center in Orlando, Florida. Like most newlyweds, we didn't have much money when we first got married. As a couple, we never made more than $40,000 a year combined when we lived in Colorado. The high school did give a small raise every year. By 1997, between marriage bonus and small raises, I was still only making around $13,000 a year teaching. There were zero benefits though, so I needed to make the National Team in wrestling so we could have the insurance that came with it.

I definitely hit the jackpot when I met Rachel. She's an awesome person and there was an immediate attraction – at least for me. The year of writing and calling eventually won her over and the attraction turned to love. There was a sweetness to her that was apparent from the first sentence she spoke to me. She saw my wrestling as a positive. She saw how I used it through the ministry I had and as a Christian. She trusted me and she is a great complement to me. She is so selfless and gracious. I'm so blessed that she came into my life.

I also quickly realized that Rachel was the person I couldn't live without. She filled a need in my life and we just really connected. Marrying her obviously was one of the best decisions I ever made.

With Rachel's support, I continued to have success in wrestling. During the time we started dating, I was pursuing my goal of making a U.S. Olympic Team.

The 1996 Olympics were approaching and they were going

## NOT ALL ROADS LEAD TO GOLD

to be held in the United States for the first time in 12 years. Atlanta was going to host the Olympic Games that year. I was ready to make a run at the U.S. Greco-Roman Olympic spot at 62 kilograms.

I advanced to the finals of the 1996 U.S. Open in Las Vegas and faced veteran Shon Lewis in the championship match. We were locked in a close match before time ran out and I earned a hard-fought victory.

My hand was raised by the referee, but unfortunately that wasn't the end of it. Lewis' coaches protested and challenged the outcome of the match. USA Wrestling officials reviewed the protest and overturned the decision three hours after my hand had been raised.

I was still at the venue when 1992 Olympic bronze medalist Chris Campbell approached me and told me the news. And I gave back the plaque I was awarded after my hand was raised in Vegas for winning the tournament.

Shon Lewis was declared the U.S. Open champion at 62 kilograms. The officials said they had made a wrong call. It was a bad deal and I didn't understand it. I ended up losing the match on a technicality. The officials called "fleeing the mat" instead of "fleeing the hold" – a distinction without a difference. The penalty is the same. They took away the point and I lost the match.

It was soul-crushing and I was pissed. Instead of celebrating, I was sitting there for hours waiting for a final verdict by faceless people on some committee. I couldn't believe they did that to me. How could you overturn the outcome of the match hours after it was over? I ended up learning a really hard lesson that day. You can't leave the outcome of a match in the hands of the referees. My club, the Sunkist Kids, filed a grievance but nothing changed. It was a huge setback in my quest to make the 1996 Olympic Team. The advantage of winning Nationals is advancing to the finals of the Trials and avoiding the challenge tournament.

The good news was I still had a chance to make the Olympic Team. I returned to training and tried to use that loss as

## *A path of persistence, faith and perseverance*

motivation to prepare for the U.S. Olympic Team Trials.

I advanced to the semifinals of the Trials before losing to Kevin Bracken, who went on to make the Olympic Team four years later. I ended up placing third overall at my first Olympic Trials in 1996. David Zuniga, who placed fourth at the World Championships in 1994, ended up winning the Trials at my weight class. He finished 10th at the 1996 Olympics.

After the Olympic Team Trials finished, I needed a wrestling break but I was back at camps because I needed money more. Ben Peterson pulled me aside and said I needed to go to Atlanta and watch the Olympics. I was incredibly resistant for many reasons. I didn't like watching wrestling, and I wanted a break. I didn't have money for tickets, I didn't have a place to stay and I hate driving.

Ben insisted it was necessary. He was persistent and pushed me to go. And then all my excuses seemed to find counters. Ethan Bosch, a close friend and fellow resident, said he would drive. Ben provided the tickets, and Rachel had relatives that lived close to Atlanta. We drove down and, again, it was great advice from Ben. Watching the Olympics, I realized these guys are beatable and I am not light years behind them. It was as if I was absorbing the great wrestling and it helped me realize the next level – the trip had elevated my wrestling.

Shortly after the Olympics, we were informed that the International Olympic Committee was reducing the number of weight classes from 10 to 8 for both Greco-Roman and freestyle wrestling.

The 57-kilogram weight class was being changed to 58 kg. And my weight class of 62 kg went up to 63 kg. I didn't think I was big enough to wrestle 63 kg, so I decided to drop down to 58 kg as the next four-year Olympic cycle began.

My natural weight was around 140 pounds, and 63 kilograms converted to 138.75 lbs. I decided to drop down to 58 kilos, which was right around 128 pounds. I was pretty lean, so it was a tough cut. But I felt like I had a better chance to excel in the lighter weight class.

## NOT ALL ROADS LEAD TO GOLD

The move to 58 kilos proved beneficial for me. I started strong the following season, advancing to the 1997 U.S. Open finals in Orlando, Florida. And I would face a familiar foe and nemesis: Dennis Hall.

Between our meetings in 1994 and 1997, Dennis had been on an amazing run. He captured a World bronze medal in 1994, won a World title in 1995 and earned an Olympic silver medal in 1996.

Unlike the previous two bouts I had against him, where he kicked the crap out of me, this bout was going right down to the wire. Dennis struck first, scoring on a hand-to-hand turn to lead 1-0. I stormed back and launched him to his back with a headlock. I had taken control of the match and grabbed a 3-1 lead midway through the bout.

My lead remained 3-1 before a frantic, wild and bizarre end to the match. I was in control in the final seconds, but I somehow found a great way to snatch defeat from the jaws of victory.

We were scrambling for position before our momentum carried us out of bounds with 12 seconds left in the match. The referee gave him a point for what is called a caution-and-1 because they said I was fleeing the mat or fleeing the hold. I'm not sure exactly why they called it, and I'm not really sure it was the right call. When we went out of bounds, Dennis immediately made the signal to the refs for a caution-and-1 and said something to the officials. And then the refs called the caution-and-1 and gave him a point. My lead was now 3-2. For any Star Wars fans, he legitimately Jedi Mind Tricked the refs.

We went back to the center of the mat. I was a little frustrated and I came at him aggressively. I had a double-underhook on Dennis, where I gained leverage with my arms under his. He countered me with a double-overhook, locking his arms over mine, and he threw me. I exposed my back to the mat and the officials awarded him three points. He won the match 5-3.

Dennis did two backflips to celebrate and I wallowed in self-pity while shaking my head in disbelief. I couldn't believe what

## A path of persistence, faith and perseverance

just happened. I was about to beat World champion and Olympic silver medalist Dennis Hall for the first time. But it didn't happen.

I blew it. I squandered a golden opportunity. My first thought was, "Are you bleeping kidding me?" All I had to do was grab his arm and run out the clock. I had the match won and let it slip away. There was a sense of frustration and disappointment. I went through the Five Stages of Grief in an endless loop for what seemed an eternity. I was angry and upset. And kicking myself for how I had wrestled in the final seconds. I lost my focus and lost the match.

I was right there. I had really closed the gap – I had Dennis Hall against the ropes and let him off. Even though it was a crushing loss, I knew there would be other opportunities. And I was confident I was ready for a breakthrough.

I didn't have much time to feel sorry for myself. I had to hit the reset button and I went right back to work. The 1997 World Team Trials were right around the corner and I would have another opportunity.

When I decided to move down to 58 kilos, a number of people questioned me about it. Why would you cut down to the weight class that Dennis Hall is in? When I came back and made the cut down a weight, people said I was crazy. My mentality was, "Why not?" I looked at it as an opportunity to go against not only one of the best Greco-Roman wrestlers in the country, but one of the best wrestlers in the World.

I felt like it would do nothing but make me a better wrestler. I went into it fully knowing what I was getting into. I enjoyed the battle. It's something where you thrive on the intensity and it was everything you ever wanted in an epic battle. I embraced the challenge and it was awesome. I loved it. Looking back now, if I had the chance, I would do it all over again.

In 1997, Dennis had earned an automatic berth into the finals of the World Team Trials by virtue of winning the U.S. Open.

I would have to win the challenge tournament, against the

## NOT ALL ROADS LEAD TO GOLD

rest of the entries in our weight class, to earn another shot at Dennis in the finals. I came out strong and determined, powering through three matches to win the challenge tournament.

Now the stage was set for me to finally earn that elusive first victory against Dennis Hall in the finals of the World Team Trials. I actually would need two wins over him to make my first World Team. We would square off in a best-of-3 three match series. The winner would advance to the World Championships in Wroclaw, Poland.

I was eager for redemption again and ready for the rematch, but so was Dennis. He was one of the best wrestlers in the world, and as you might expect from someone of his caliber, he had made adjustments after our last match.

He swept me in the finals of the World Team Trials. He beat me 3-0 in the first match and 5-0 in the second match. Dennis was better in par terre wrestling where you would try to turn your opponent down on the mat. He was able to turn me and that was the difference.

The loss in the 1997 Trials dropped my career record against Dennis Hall to 0-6 at that point. Did I have second thoughts about dropping down to his weight class? Not at all. Dennis had beaten me again, but I absolutely felt like I was on the right track. I had closed the gap against Dennis. There was a progression there and that was a positive for me. I obviously wasn't winning against him and I hadn't arrived yet, but I had become a better wrestler. It gave me something to build on. I was having good results – I just wasn't quite there yet against Dennis.

I went on to win a silver medal at the 1997 Pan American Championships and followed by capturing a bronze medal at the Pytlasinski tournament, the pre-World tournament that Dennis decided to skip, in Poland. Those were important tournaments for me as I gained valuable experience competing against top international opponents.

As the No. 2 guy at my weight class, I earned a trip to the 1997 World Championships in Poland as a training partner for the U.S. team. That was a great experience for me. I was able to train

## *A path of persistence, faith and perseverance*

with the American team, and I also was able to observe the foreign athletes who were competing. I watched the tournament and studied the wrestlers. It was a great learning experience for me and it provided me with motivation to want to compete in the World Championships. I knew exactly the level of wrestling that I was shooting for.

Dennis Hall finished sixth at the 1997 World Championships, ending his impressive three-year run of medaling at either the Worlds or Olympics.

I was still No. 2 on the U.S. ladder at 58 kilograms. It was the highest I had been, but I still wasn't happy. I was training to be the best wrestler on the planet. And I wasn't going to stop until I reached the top.

## CHAPTER 5
# BREAKING THROUGH

My excitement level was sky-high entering the 1998 season. Even though I was still coming up short in my quest to make my first U.S. Senior World Team, I had continued to improve. I had come close to knocking off long-time nemesis Dennis Hall, but I kept falling short. Beating Dennis obviously would be no small feat. He had won a World title and an Olympic silver medal.

Dennis was the gold standard for Greco-Roman wrestling in the United States. He was one of the best pound-for-pound wrestlers on the entire planet. But I also knew I was capable after nearly defeating him in 1997.

I was wrestling well going into the U.S. Nationals. After pissing away a six-point lead in the finals, I placed second in a tournament in Norway. I wasn't overly pleased with the officiating. Andy Seras, a Greco Olympian and my coach on this winter tour, helped me hit the reset button. He offered some solid advice and calmed me down. I responded the following week and won the Swedish Grand Prix.

Winning in Sweden was a big deal for me. I beat Olympic freestyle silver medalist Armen Mkrtchyan of Armenia 3-1 in overtime. It proved to me I could compete with the best guys in the World. I was beating top foreign opponents, and finally won one of the biggest Greco events of the year.

I had another big win that season. I won the Pan American

## NOT ALL ROADS LEAD TO GOLD

Championships in 1998. I defeated Roberto Monzon of Cuba 4-1 in the finals of the Pan American Championships in Winnipeg, Canada. He was a two-time Junior World champion and went on to have a superb career on the Senior level. He won World bronze medals in 2001 and 2002 before winning a World silver medal in 2003. He followed by winning an Olympic silver medal in 2004.

I ended up with a 4-4 record against him in my career. Monzon was a dynamic, talented and gifted wrestler. Like many of the Cubans, he was a tremendous athlete with lightning-quick speed. He also had an iron set of lungs on him. He wrestled hard and it was difficult to break his spirit. I could typically wear opponents down with my high level of stamina and conditioning, but Monzon was a fighter. We had some great battles.

Beating Monzon was a good stepping stone to where I ultimately wanted to be. Typically, it was the U.S. against Cuba in the Pan Ams, although a few years later that changed with Cuban coaches helping with other South American countries.

I was having really good results internationally and I felt like I was wrestling at a high level early in the 1998 season. That was good news going into the important domestic competitions that year.

I received my next opportunity to wrestle Dennis Hall in the 1998 U.S. Open. We met in the finals and he beat me again by a 5-0 score. It was frustrating because I felt a step behind the whole match. Making matters worse was what Dennis said in his post-finals interview. He said he had not been training that hard before our finals match in 1997 and that was why our match was so close.

It was crazy how many times we would face each other, but he was the guy I had to go through if I was going to achieve my goals.

The U.S. Open was another setback for me, but I still had time to regroup and prepare to meet him later in the year. Dennis suffered an injury shortly before the World Team Trials. As the No. 1 guy, he was granted an extension since he had won the U.S. Open. The delay also benefited me. I had broken my big toe

## A path of persistence, faith and perseverance

wrestling at a camp for Ben and wasn't 100 percent. I was able to sit out of the challenge tournament and only had to wrestle the finals against a much weaker opponent.

I won the World Team Trials and then earned an opportunity to wrestle Dennis in a Special Wrestle-Off at a later date. We would meet at the U.S. Air Force Academy in Colorado Springs.

In the first match of the best-of-3 series, I took a 2-0 lead on a gut wrench. It was the only time in 23 matches that I ever executed that move on Dennis. I had the lead late in the match, but without the required three points by either opponent, we went into overtime. Ten seconds into the overtime, I relaxed for a second. And you can't relax against a wrestler of Dennis Hall's caliber. He scored a quick one-point takedown and then trapped my arm to my side before turning me for a two-point gut-wrench to win the match. I lost 3-2.

It was an unwelcome pattern that was developing in my matches against Dennis. It was the third time he had come from behind to defeat me. I was a guy known for being in excellent physical condition. I typically was strongest near the end of the match where my stamina was superior to my opponents. But Dennis was a never surrender athlete. He never quit, no matter what. He was a tremendous competitor who always expected to win.

My coach, Anatoly Petrosyan, and I walked a lap outside as I cooled down from the exasperating loss. In classic Anatoly fashion, he asked, "Jim, you had bird, why you let bird go."

"Anatoly, I wanted to kill the bird, I have no idea why I let him go," I replied in frustration.

Some of his Russian analogies were lost on me. Losing that first match the way I did definitely lit a fire under me for the second match. I responded and beat him for the first time in my career.

I earned a hard-fought 3-2 win. I had finally beaten Dennis Hall. I felt like I had just climbed to the top of Pikes Peak. Eleven long years since our first match. I no longer felt like the one-legged man at a butt-kicking contest.

## NOT ALL ROADS LEAD TO GOLD

I didn't do any wild or crazy celebrations because we still had another match to wrestle. But it was still a super euphoric experience. After losing the first eight times we had wrestled, I had finally defeated him.

People were coming up and congratulating me. They were telling me I will never lose to him again. But I had poked the bear. And my sense of euphoria was short-lived.

I entered the third and deciding match with the same game plan. I felt like I had him right where I wanted. But Dennis, as he always did, came back strong. To say he wasn't happy about losing to me is a gross understatement. Imagine, if you will, tossing dynamite into a dormant volcano. Then thinking, 'Oh crap, I just tossed dynamite into a volcano.' And not being able to leave. He was a rage wrestler, and I had just fed his rage.

He took me down, he turned me and he threw me. Over and over and over again. It was ugly – probably the ugliest loss of my 16 career losses to him.

I fell behind early and it snowballed against me. Losing to me lit a fire under Dennis and he soundly defeated me by a score of 10-0.

It was a little smorgasbord of Greco for him, and he was going to take a little bit of this and a little bit of that. He roundhouse kicked my dreams of a second win into the future. I walked off the mat again in disbelief. This was not the way it was supposed to happen.

It was disappointing and I was down for a little bit. What made the whole situation more embarrassing was that a group from my church and high school came to watch. I was at home in Colorado Springs and people were excited to watch me wrestle. And then that happened. One of the sweetest women I know from church came up after Dennis finished crushing me and celebrating and said to me, "He just makes me so mad." I knew the feeling.

I had to hit the reset button once again. It was a positive that I had finally won a match against Dennis Hall. There was a crack in the wall with a little bit of daylight finally seeping through. But

## *A path of persistence, faith and perseverance*

he was still the man and still the No. 1 guy in the USA.

I was right there with the best guys in the World, but I couldn't make the American team by only beating Dennis once. I had to do it twice. On the same day.

The same scenario unfolded again in 1999. Dennis beat me in the finals of the U.S. Open before we met again in the finals of the World Team Trials. He took control in the first match of the best-of- series. He threw me early in the match before I lost 4-3.

I came back to earn a 1-0 win in the second match. Much like the year before, he came back strong and beat me 8-0 in the third match. He thumped me in the match that mattered most.

I once again was No. 2 on the U.S. ladder. I had earned another match win over Dennis, but I was still 2-12 in my career against him. It wasn't as bad as 1998, but it was still super frustrating to lose to him in the 1999 World Team Trials. The frustration was also starting to build and take a toll on my dad, who had been following me everywhere for competitions.

After the third match, Rachel and my dad were walking back with me to the hotel and Rachel let me know my dad's frustration had bubbled to the surface. Apparently, Dennis celebrated and yelled in victory at the crowd. In a fit of annoyance, my dad stood up and with a single finger and let Dennis Hall know he was number 1. I talked to my dad a short time later.

"Dad, did you flip Dennis off after the last match?" I asked.

He sheepishly replied that he did and went on to say, "that Dennis makes me so mad."

"Try wrestling him, dad," I replied. "I get it, but we cannot lose control."

This was out of character for my dad. Normally, he just cheered and hugged regardless of winning and losing. But even the calmest of my fans felt the frustration. In the end, he promised it would never happen again.

I was still wrestling well internationally which made losing to Dennis even more baffling. I was doing everything right, or so I thought. Dennis was skipping the overseas tournaments, and I

## NOT ALL ROADS LEAD TO GOLD

was gobbling up everything he skipped. I won the Dave Schultz tournament and the Poland Open that year. I was winning overseas against quality foreign opponents.

I knew I was capable of winning a World or Olympic medal, but I had to make the American team first. I was wrestling at a high level and I had made adjustments with my wrestling.

I was eating the right foods and getting the right amount of sleep. I was listening to my coaches. I had great training partners. And I was competing in 40-60 matches in a year.

I was making improvements, but something was missing and I thought I needed to do more. I realized I needed to make some more changes if I was going to reach my goals. Winning and losing do not define us, they direct us.

CHAPTER 6
# OLYMPIC DREAMS

There is something special about an Olympic year. And the year 2000 was no exception. When the calendar flipped to January 1, 2000, I was like a kid in a candy store. I couldn't wait to make a run at earning a berth on the United States Olympic Team.

I would celebrate my 30th birthday in June of that year, but I still felt like I hadn't reached my peak as an athlete.

I had been very close to reaching my goal of making a U.S. World or Olympic Team in Greco-Roman wrestling, but had continued to fall just short.

I placed second to Dennis Hall at the U.S. World Team Trials for three straight years from 1997-99. But now it was time for me to reverse my fortunes.

I had won one match against Dennis in both 1998 and 1999. And those were big steps for me. But I knew I really needed to step it up in 2000.

Dennis Hall was a two-time Olympian and he had captured a silver medal at the 1996 Olympic Games. He was the No. 1 guy and he was driven to make his third straight Olympic Team.

My objective was to prevent that from happening. It obviously wasn't going to be easy. Beating Dennis wasn't my only concern. The U.S. still needed to qualify for the Olympic Games in my weight class of 58 kilograms/127.75 pounds.

There was definitely a sense of urgency for the United

## NOT ALL ROADS LEAD TO GOLD

States Greco-Roman squad. We didn't have that many weights qualified and that was a major cause for concern.

Many people aren't aware that you actually have to qualify to compete in the Olympic Games. There is a process where you have to earn a spot in the Olympic field before you can actually compete and pursue a medal on the sport's biggest stage.

The field for the Olympics was limited to 20 wrestlers per weight class and countries had to earn spots through qualifying events.

At the World Championships, where any country could compete, there might be closer to 40 wrestlers entered in a weight class.

There was a system of qualifying for the Olympic Games in wrestling that involved numerous steps.

The first Olympic qualifier came at the 1999 World Championships. The top six finishers in each weight class at that event would qualify their country for the Olympics. That was the main qualifier. If you didn't qualify there, the pressure would magnify and intensify for countries trying to earn spots at the world's most prestigious sporting event.

Dennis Hall had been highly successful at the international level, winning a World title and an Olympic silver medal. But he hadn't been quite as successful in this four-year Olympic cycle.

That trend continued when Hall went 0-2 at the 1999 World Championships, so Team USA still had to qualify for the 2000 Olympic Games.

The next step was a series of Olympic qualifying tournaments. In 2000, there were five tournaments set up for athletes from the countries who didn't qualify at the World Championships. They took place from January through March of that year.

A country could wrestle in all five events, but only three events were used in the total. The top seven finishers in each weight class qualified their nation for the Olympics.

The first qualifier was in Italy and Dennis was scheduled to compete at 58 kilograms. I wasn't originally slated to go, but our

## A path of persistence, faith and perseverance

top two guys were sidelined at the next weight class above me at 63 kg/138.75 pounds.

U.S. National Coach Steve Fraser approached me the week of the event and asked if I would be able to compete. It was a last-minute decision, but I didn't have much of a choice. I had to go. Our country needed me. I flew to Italy on a Thursday, weighed in on Friday, competed on Saturday and flew home Sunday.

The good news was that I didn't have to cut any weight and I had a good tournament. I placed third for the U.S. at 63 kg and earned us 23 valuable points in the first of five qualifying tournaments. Dennis placed 12th at 58 kg.

The bad news was I dislocated one of my ribs. Making matters worse, our U.S. doctor didn't have much experience with this type of injury and was trying to push the rib back into place. Short of surgery and wiring it back into place, the rib would stay out. But he kept pushing – that made the pain even more excruciating.

This was going to be a long, tough, grueling year especially with the qualifiers being held every two weeks. That left little recovery time even without an injury.

Dennis Hall was scheduled to wrestle the first and fourth qualifiers, and I was scheduled to wrestle at the second and third qualifiers. I moved back down to my weight class of 58 kg and competed for the U.S.

Rib still out, I placed third in France and ninth in Uzbekistan. That put the U.S. in seventh place after the first three Olympic qualifiers.

Dennis wrestled in the next qualifier in Colorado Springs and placed second. Unfortunately, he lost to Rifat Yildiz of Germany and we dropped to eighth in the standings at 58 kg.
I was called on for the fifth Olympic qualifier of the series. I won the final qualifier in Egypt. Even though I won, there were not enough entrants to improve our total.

We had traveled all over the globe, but we had come up just short of the Olympics. It was a tough blow, but we would still have one more opportunity to qualify for the Olympics at the Pan

## NOT ALL ROADS LEAD TO GOLD

American Championships.

Before that, the U.S. Open was held in April. That was another important event because the champion would receive an automatic berth into the finals of the Olympic Trials. The champion also would go to the Pan Ams for the last chance to qualify for the Olympic Games.

The U.S. Open unfolded in familiar fashion with Dennis and I hammering our way to the finals. And once again, I came up short in a knock-down, drag-out brawl. Dennis Hall scored a 4-3 victory over me.

He had landed a berth in the finals of the Olympic Trials. And I had finished second at the U.S. Open for the fifth consecutive year.

Winning the U.S. Open was significant for Hall, but it wouldn't have mattered if we didn't qualify the weight class for the Olympic Games.

Our final chance to qualify for the Olympics came at the Pan American Championships on May 19, 2000, in Cali, Colombia. We needed to win that event to qualify for the Olympics at 58 kilograms.

Since he won the U.S. Open, Dennis Hall was picked to represent the American team at the Pan Am Championships. Dennis advanced to the finals against a talented young opponent – two-time Junior World champion Roberto Monzon of Cuba. The pressure was enormous with an Olympic berth at stake.

The pressure was heightened even more as the Hall-Monzon match went into overtime. As the seconds ticked closer to the end, Dennis was behind in a tight match. With a second left and a heroic last effort, he scored a clutch takedown with one second left in overtime to earn a dramatic victory over the Cuban.

After all we had been through, with all of the qualifiers and everything, we made the Olympic Games by one second.

Dennis Hall had delivered. As I experienced first-hand, Dennis had a penchant for pulling out big wins in the final seconds.

Monzon went on to win three World medals (a silver and

## *A path of persistence, faith and perseverance*

two bronze) and an Olympic silver medal in the next cycle from 2001-04. The Cuban was really talented, but Dennis had come through to win a huge, pressure-packed match against him with the stakes extremely high.

I was back at the U.S. Olympic Training Center in Colorado Springs waiting for word on if we had qualified.

There was no live video streaming or social media back then. We didn't have the modern technology to find out immediately what happened.

Word finally reached us by phone from the Pan Ams. Dennis Hall had qualified the weight class for the Olympic Games. When I received the news, I smiled and pumped my fist. I thanked God. And I thanked Dennis Hall. My Olympic dream was still alive.

It obviously was a huge relief. I was stressing about it. It was a helpless feeling, waiting to hear the results. Obviously, I was pulling for Dennis to get the weight qualified. I would've had to either move up or move down a weight class if we didn't get into the Olympics at 58 kilos.

We were one second away from not wrestling in Sydney, but Dennis came through. I was a huge Dennis Hall fan, at least for that day.

I can't emphasize it enough. It is really difficult just to make it into the Olympics. There are World and Olympic medalists sitting at home during every Olympic Games. The field was only 20 guys per weight class (it was down to 16 in 2020). It is very difficult just to get into the Olympic tournament. Not a lot of people understand. It's a brutal, soul-crushing process.

There is tremendous pressure to qualify for the Olympics. It's enormous. When you are out there, it's all resting on your shoulders. You are not only trying to qualify the weight class for yourself, but for your country. The pressure was finally off. The U.S. was in.

We were one of 20 nations who had earned a berth at 58 kg for the 2000 Olympic Games. Dennis Hall had just qualified the U.S. for the Olympics, but the good news for me was he still had to make the American team.

## NOT ALL ROADS LEAD TO GOLD

The 2000 United States Olympic Team Trials would be held in late June at Reunion Arena in Dallas, Texas. It was held at the home basketball arena for the NBA's Dallas Mavericks. It was a nice arena that seated 15,000 fans.

During the time between the U.S. Open and the Olympic Trials, I realized I needed to make some changes. I had been overtraining. I had coaches who pointed it out to me and I listened.

When I was younger, I didn't really believe there was such a thing as overtraining. You always wanted to do more and not take much time off. It was the old-school Dan Gable philosophy of believing you could never train enough in your quest to be the best.

But my coaches knew I needed to back off the gas pedal. And they were right. I still trained hard, but I trained smarter. I took more breaks and eased up on the intensity of my workouts in the last few weeks before competition.

I gave my body more of a chance to recover. I felt fresher and had more energy. The plan to train smarter was working. I started learning the importance of less is more.

I entered the 2000 Olympic Trials as the No. 1 seed for the challenge tournament. Dennis Hall sat out and was already in the best-of-3 finals because he had won the U.S. Open. Since I placed second at the Open, I drew the top seed for the challenge tournament.

I was eager for another chance to face Hall, but I had work to do first. I had to win three matches in the challenge tournament.

I powered through my first two matches before I met veteran Duaine Martin in the finals. Martin was an experienced wrestler who had been around even longer than I had. He was a tough, hard-nosed competitor who wrestled for the U.S. Marine Corps.

Duaine and I had wrestled a few times in the past four years. He was normally the No. 3 or No. 4 seed at Nationals. He was the guy, that if you had an off day, he could beat you. And this was an Olympic year. Crazy things happen at every Olympic Trials.

## *A path of persistence, faith and perseverance*

I was trying to turn him with a gut-wrench, got loose, and he countered by stepping over me. He caught me on my back briefly and scored three points in that sequence. I quickly fell behind 3-0. I was in a big hole initially.

I was able to fight off my back and regroup. Luckily, it was early in the match and I had plenty of time to rally. I kept my cool and my composure, and I quickly gained control. I won the match 9-3.

I captured three straight matches to win the challenge tournament and the fans cheered after each of my wins. The crowds aren't always huge for Greco-Roman wrestling, but the fan support for all three styles was awesome in Dallas.

There were as many as 9,000 fans in attendance for the sessions there and it was amazing wrestling in that kind of an atmosphere.

I had achieved the first part of my objective in Texas. I had advanced to the finals of the 2000 Olympic Trials. Now came the hard part. I had to beat Dennis Hall to make the U.S. team. Twice. I knew it was going to be a battle. And it did not disappoint.

Those matches with Dennis were some of the most challenging – physically and mentally – I ever wrestled. It was a knock-down, all-out brawl. We did not stop pounding on each other the entire time.

It had been a grueling year for both of us. I had wrestled in four of the five Olympic qualification tournaments and also wrestled in the U.S. Open.

Dennis had also competed frequently and had delivered in the Pan Ams to qualify the U.S. for the Olympics. I had been in some high pressure matches, but none measured up to these.

The Olympic Games were the pinnacle in our sport and that's the goal I had my sights set on since I was in high school. I was two wins away from realizing my dream and making a United States Olympic Team.

But my long-time nemesis was standing in my way. At this point, I had a 3-13 record against him over 12 years – the bulk of those matches occurred in the last four years.

## NOT ALL ROADS LEAD TO GOLD

*Right:* Ready for battle during my freshman year of high school.

*Below:* Standing atop the podium after winning USA Wrestling's Northern Plains event at 99 pounds.

86

*A path of persistence, faith and perseverance*

With my brother, Alan, and our high school coach,
Bob Carlson.

Working for a fall at USA Wrestling's Junior Nationals.

# NOT ALL ROADS LEAD TO GOLD

*Above:* Having my hand raised after a win at the Junior Nationals in Cedar Falls, Iowa.

A moment of reflection when I made the state finals in 1987.

*A path of persistence, faith and perseverance*

Reacting after winning a Wisconsin high school state championship at 112 pounds in 1987.

Trying to gain leverage against Dennis Hall during the 1988 Wisconsin high school state finals.

# NOT ALL ROADS LEAD TO GOLD

Looking for an edge from the top as Hall tries to slow me down.

Standing next to Dennis Hall after falling to him in the 1988 state finals in Wisconsin.

*A path of persistence, faith and perseverance*

*Above:* With my father and brother at a graduation party. My dad drove us to a lot of tournaments.

During my days at Maranatha, where I thrived under the guidance of Olympic gold medalist Ben Peterson.

# NOT ALL ROADS LEAD TO GOLD

Winning a gold medal at the 1998 Pan Ams.

*Below:* With my mother and stepdad. My mom encouraged me to pursue my Olympic dreams after college.

*A path of persistence, faith and perseverance*

Dennis Hall and I had some big matches over the years, but none bigger than when we met in the 2000 Olympic Trials in Dallas.

Trying to fight off the attack of Hall at the 2000 Trials.

# NOT ALL ROADS LEAD TO GOLD

Battling for position against Hall at the Trials.

*Below:* Celebrating after finally beating Dennis Hall in the finals of the 2000 Olympic Team Trials.

*A path of persistence, faith and perseverance*

*Above:* Earning a win over Armenia in my Olympic debut in 2000 in Sydney, Australia.

With my awesome wife, Rachel, during the 2000 Olympic Games.

## NOT ALL ROADS LEAD TO GOLD

With my coach and mentor, Ben Peterson, at the Olympics.

Hanging out with family and friends during the Olympic Games.

*A path of persistence, faith and perseverance*

With teammate Ethan Bosch at the 2002 World Cup.

Earning a victory at the World Championships.

## NOT ALL ROADS LEAD TO GOLD

The U.S. Greco-Roman squad that competed at the 2003 Pan Am Games. I'm the guy with the beard on the right side of the bottom row.

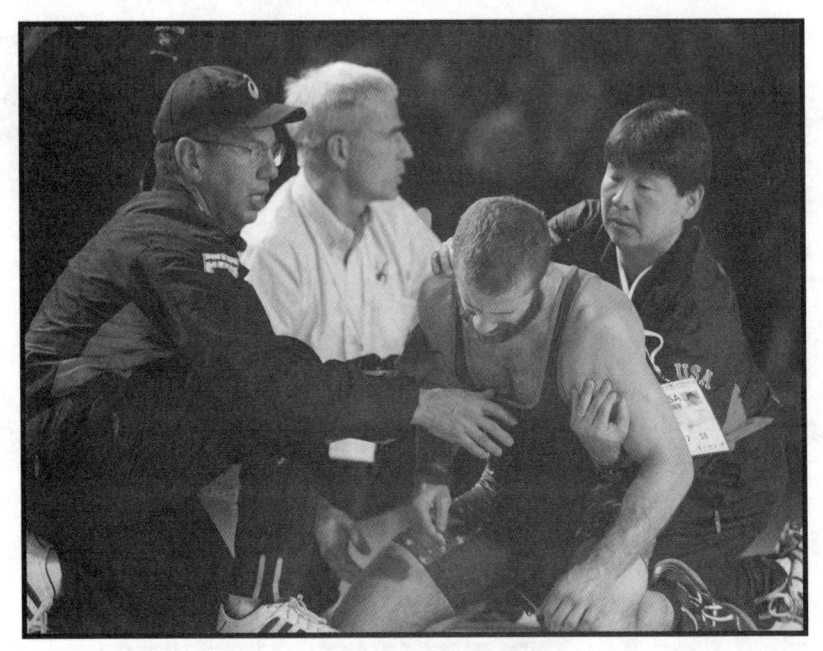

Down on the mat after injuring my shoulder in the semifinals of the 2003 World Championships in Creteil, France.

*A path of persistence, faith and perseverance*

With U.S. National Coach Steve Fraser after being injured.

Walking off the mat with Fraser after being forced to default a match for the first time in my career.

## NOT ALL ROADS LEAD TO GOLD

I competed in my second Olympics in 2004 with this tough group of guys. I'm in the middle of the back row next to Dennis Hall.

Wrestling at the 2004 Olympic Games in Athens, Greece.

*A path of persistence, faith and perseverance*

Trying to control Joe Betterman during the finals of the 2008 U.S. Open in Las Vegas.

Coming out of retirement after three years away included its share of challenges.

## NOT ALL ROADS LEAD TO GOLD

Looking for a turn while battling Betterman, one of the wrestlers I coached at Northern Michigan.

Trying to break free from a front headlock at the Open.

*A path of persistence, faith and perseverance*

Wrestlers end up in the most awkward positions sometimes.

Earning points with a turn during my comeback to wrestling in 2008.

# NOT ALL ROADS LEAD TO GOLD

*Above:* Looking for big points in my match against Betterman.

Winning the 2008 U.S. Open, an event I finished second in way too many times in my career.

*A path of persistence, faith and perseverance*

Coach Ivan Ivanov and I with 2008 Olympic Trials champions Spenser Mango, Joe Betterman and Adam Wheeler in Las Vegas.

# NOT ALL ROADS LEAD TO GOLD

Northern Michigan alum and 2008 Olympic bronze medalist Adam Wheeler. Adam got hot at the right time in 2008.

I spent a lot of time training with Spenser Mango, a two-time Olympian who was great to work with.

*A path of persistence, faith and perseverance*

Harry Lester was the best wrestler I ever coached. He was a two-time World medalist who should've been a World champion in 2007.

One of the biggest success stories to come out of the USOEC was Andy Bisek, a walk-on who won two World medals and became an Olympian.

# NOT ALL ROADS LEAD TO GOLD

Following the action during a match while coaching at Wheaton College.

Letting the referee know that was a takedown.

*A path of persistence, faith and perseverance*

Providing feedback for Wheaton wrestler Carlos Fuentez after he won the Pete Willson Invitational. Fuentez placed second at the NCAA Division III tournament in 2018.

Providing instruction during a camp in the summer of 2021.

# NOT ALL ROADS LEAD TO GOLD

With my beautiful wife while attending the wedding of one of my former wrestlers in 2021.

Fun photo for our family Christmas card in 2020

*A path of persistence, faith and perseverance*

My nephew, Caleb, did this portrait of me in 2021.

## NOT ALL ROADS LEAD TO GOLD

There was an enormous amount of pressure going into that best-of-3 match series against Dennis Hall, but I was ready.

I walked onto the main arena floor for the first match of the final-round series. Hall of Fame announcer Ed Aliverti introduced us to the crowd.

"Now wrestling in the Greco-Roman finals at 58 kilograms, from the Sunkist Kids, Jim Gruenwald."

I ran onto the mat and bounced lightly on my feet.

"And his opponent," Aliverti announced. "Also wrestling for the Sunkist Kids, Dennis Hall."

I actually had a smile on my face just before the first match. USA Coach Steve Fraser was always preaching to us to enjoy and embrace the battle. And that's what I did.

I was going into the biggest matches of my life and I had a smile on his face. But I wasn't smiling for long.

The crowd cheered as we walked toward the center of the mat and shook hands. The whistle blew and the match was underway.

It was the first match of the finals of the Olympic Trials. And I had to be prepared to possibly wrestle three matches against one of the best competitors on the planet.

I came out aggressively, but I was pushing so hard that Dennis saw an opening. Lateral drop alert. I went flying through the air. He launched me. He wasn't messing around and took a quick 3-0 lead.

Dennis had already made Olympic Teams in 1992 and 1996. He won an Olympic silver medal in 1996 and he was determined to make his third straight U.S. team.

I came back to the center after being thrown and I was smiling again. That's a strange reaction to have after being launched, but I knew it was still early in the match. I was down 3-0, but I was confident I could fight my way back. I did fight back, drawing within a point before losing the match by a 3-2 score. At the very end of the bout, I snapped him down to the mat and just missed going behind him for a takedown. I blew a chance to score at the end. But I also blew it by getting thrown early in

## A path of persistence, faith and perseverance

the match. That's what really cost me.

I had lost the first match and now the odds were stacked against me. He only needed one more win to make the Olympic Team. And I needed two.

I was exhausted after that first match, but I know he was tired as well. I could feel it. We had a really intense match. We were both physical wrestlers who liked to push the pace. It was an all-out battle when we competed.

After the match, Ben Peterson was speaking with me in the warmup area. Dennis, coming from the opposite tunnel, was upset about something and we heard him yelling. One of the tournament workers looked at us and said, "Didn't he just win? What is he so angry about?"

I had known Dennis for many years and knew that his intensity often presented itself as anger. Ben wasn't trying to intentionally gawk, but he was staring. Dennis saw my coach looking at him. And Dennis started chirping at Ben.

Still hopped up on adrenaline, my own anger buried at an unknown level, I immediately gave Dennis some unsolicited, sarcastic advice.

"You should probably save your energy," I called out to Dennis. "We have two more matches."

"One more!" he fired back

"Two more!" I replied.

That moment was out of character for me. Emotions were running high after that first match and everyone just needed to calm down.

A few minutes after the exchange in the hallway, I had calmed down. I walked over to Dennis and said, "Hey, I'm sorry, let's just keep it on the mat."

He looked up and said, "Yeah."

I had to regain my focus. I hit the reset the button and came out determined in the second match against Dennis Hall. I had to win the next match, or I was done. Fortunately, I wrestled really well.

I took him down twice with the same move, once each

## NOT ALL ROADS LEAD TO GOLD

period, to grab a 2-0 lead. I had a two-on-one with both of my hands locked around his arm. I used that to step in between his legs and grab his waist before taking him to the mat. I stayed on the attack and he was put down for passivity. I scored a point on a lift after he was put down. I controlled the match and I earned a solid 3-0 victory.

As time ran out, the big crowd cheered. They were knowledgeable fans and they knew a win over Dennis Hall was no small feat.

I was really fired up when I won that match. I was relieved because our series wasn't over. I had forced a third and deciding match. I was exhausted because it was another brawl, but I also knew I had time to recover. I knew I had to regroup because I had one more match to go. And I still had a chance to make the 2000 United States Olympic Team.

In 1998 and 1999, we were in the same position at the World Team Trials. Both of those times, Hall stomped me in the third and deciding match to make the World Team. People were probably expecting him to smash me again. I had that in my mind. I knew he was going to come at me hard in the third match. I'm sure people were thinking that this was Dennis Hall and he wasn't going to be denied. They had observed a clear pattern for two years.

We walked onto the mat for Bout No. 3. The third match was probably the craziest one of all. As expected, Dennis charged out aggressively. At one point, we kept wrestling six feet out of the circle onto the carpet on the platform. I hadn't been called for passivity in either of the first matches, but that changed in the third match. He forced a passivity call against me and was able to score a one-point gut-wrench after I was put in the down position.

I came back and forced a passivity call against him. He was put down and I went for a gut-wrench and tried to turn him. But he stepped over me. As I scrambled to avoid being put on my back, I attempted a duck under from my knees. Dennis transitioned to a front headlock and scored two points right before the buzzer. I was down 3-0 after the first period. I thought,

## A path of persistence, faith and perseverance

"Dang, here we go again." I actually started walking to the wrong corner.

Reversing course, I went back to my corner and started having a moment of reflection. I was like, "God, if you want me on this Olympic Team it's going to have to be you because I keep blowing it." Here I am in the same situation where I'm about to lose the third match to Dennis Hall for the third straight year. I said a short prayer and I went back to the mat with a sense of peace.

The second period started and we were banging away at each other while trying to gain an edge. I snapped him down in a front headlock position and he went to high dive me with a body lock. He got his hips too far forward and I steamrolled right over the top of him. His back exposed to the mat and I was about to score big points against him. He started screaming that I hit a leg foul. And in Greco-Roman, we couldn't use our legs to trip an opponent. In that sequence, I had picked him up and lifted him while throwing him out of bounds.

Head official Rick Tucci, along with referees Tom Clark and Dave Errett, looked at a video replay of the sequence. They gave me three points for taking him to his back and gave me one point for the lift. That gave me a 4-3 lead. There was still over two minutes left in the match. We went back to hammering away at each other. Knowing the dangers of wrestling Dennis, I kept the wrestling to short underhooks and heavy snaps. Learning from past matches, any time we went out of bounds it was with him going first.

With a minute left, I snapped him down again in the exact same scenario and spun behind him for a takedown. I was up 5-3. Then I lifted and threw him for a point out of bounds to go up 6-3. He was put down in par terre again and tried to sit through and exposed his own back to give me another two points.

I was up 8-3. It was the first time I had ever wrestled Dennis Hall where I felt him break. He was such a strong wrestler, but I definitely felt him weaken late in this match.

The final seconds ticked off the clock. And the horn

# NOT ALL ROADS LEAD TO GOLD

sounded. I had won the match 8-3. An announcement came over the loudspeakers as the fans gave me a standing ovation.

"And your 2000 United States Olympian at 58 kilograms," Aliverti announced. "Jim Gruenwald!"

My wife was there to share it with me, but watching me wrestle was stressful for her. In the beginning, Rachel struggled with watching me compete. The first time my name was announced at the 1996 Olympic Trials, she almost vomited. But over the years, she was able to enjoy the earlier matches in a tournament. However, the matches against Dennis Hall carried emotional weight she couldn't carry.

These matches were beyond intense, and she had spent all three hiding and praying in the bathroom. The emotions surrounding our battles were too much. In the last match, a female security guard that she befriended was watching for her, and with 10 seconds left in the match let Rachel know, "He's going to win!!" My wife was able to walk out and see the last few seconds of the match. And she witnessed my hand being raised in victory.

I had made the 2000 United States Olympic Team. I pointed up to God. My hand was raised and I remember bowing to the crowd on each side of the arena as they stood and cheered.

Chills ran down my body. It was a feeling of euphoria. I had just defeated my nemesis to make the Olympic Team. I was excited, elated and relieved.

I finally did it. My Olympic dreams were finally coming true. Or were they? Immediately after the match, Dennis Hall approached the scorer's table. He was at the table screaming at the referees – he wanted to protest the match. He felt like there was a leg foul in the match. He thought I had illegally tripped him when I scored on the four-point move in the second period.

Dennis protested the third and final match in Dallas, but the Protest Committee for the Olympic Team Trials upheld the decision.

Hall then appealed the Protest Committee's decision to USA Wrestling's Greco-Roman Sport Committee. That body agreed

## *A path of persistence, faith and perseverance*

with the Protest Committee's decision on July 19, 2000, denying Hall's appeal.

After that, Dennis took it one step further. He filed a Demand for Arbitration, but the arbitrator decided not to overturn the decision.

The entire time, I kept thinking they were going to overturn this the way they had done to me at the 1996 U.S. Open. Instead of hours, now the fear was the match would be overturned weeks later.

We were both still training because Dennis was still trying to get the decision overturned. I knew when I left Dallas that I still wasn't 100 percent on the Olympic Team. I felt helpless throughout the whole process.

That same year, two of my friends, Matt Lindland and Keith Sieracki were in a similar battle. Matt Lindland won his case to have Keith Sieracki's Olympic Trials win over him overturned. So that added to my anxiety because that was going on at the same time as when Dennis Hall was protesting my win over him. Lindland didn't win the Olympic Trials, but an arbitrator ruled he would wrestle a match against Sieracki in Colorado Springs. Lindland won the match to make the Olympic Team and he went on to win an Olympic silver medal in 2000.

During that six-week period of uncertainty with all of the appeals, it somewhat tainted the experience for me. I wasn't able to experience the joy of making the Olympic Team like I should have. I wasn't able to celebrate with my wife and my family because of the protests. There was a lot going on.

It was a long and stress-filled six weeks. I was still training and preparing for the Olympics, but I was worried I was going to lose my spot. There was a ton of anxiety. My heart was always in my throat. This was my dream. I had won the Olympic Trials and my hand was raised, but I didn't know if I was going to be allowed to wrestle in the Olympic Games. I tried to immerse myself in my training, but I'm human. I was praying and hoping for the best. I had been training my entire life for this and I knew it might get taken away from me.

## NOT ALL ROADS LEAD TO GOLD

When it was finally official, my wife and I were with my brother-in-law and sister-in-law in Pennsylvania. I received a call and then USA Wrestling sent me a fax with the news. The arbitrator ruled in favor of USA Wrestling and in favor of me.

The ruling came on Aug. 7, 2000, nearly six weeks after the Olympic Trials. USA Wrestling was notified that Hall's arbitration claim had been denied.

The fax read:

*The Award of the Arbitrator provides that Jim Gruenwald is the representative at 58 kg/127.75 pounds in Greco-Roman wrestling on the U.S. Olympic Team.*

Finally, the long, stressful and frustrating ordeal was over. I had a sense of relief, but part of me felt like I was cheated out of the excitement from making the Olympic Team.

But I also knew Keith Sieracki had won the Olympic Trials, and he wasn't going to the Olympics. I can't imagine how awful that was for Keith and his family.

My family, particularly my parents, had been really upset during the appeals process. They were angry and frustrated, and that was understandable. It was a difficult situation. At the same time, my parents also were supportive and wanted the best for me.

My wife wasn't happy either, but she didn't show it. Rachel was supportive and tried to keep things positive. She was really a rock for me. She helped me keep my sanity and keep me grounded. I'm so appreciative of her and her calming influence. It was a difficult, difficult time and she really helped me in so many ways.

I wish I could claim that I wasn't on an emotional roller coaster. I wish I could claim that I was spiritually strong enough to be unflappable during the emotional storm; that my trust in God was enough. But I wasn't. I had moments of anxiety. Nothing close to real clinical depression, but there was an always present ache in the pit of my stomach. Don't misunderstand me, my faith helped, and I cannot imagine going through those weeks without a strong faith. But it did expose some growth needs in

## *A path of persistence, faith and perseverance*

my life and faith.

When we found out I was officially on the team, I shared a long embrace with my wife. The weight of the world had been lifted off my shoulders.

I had finally achieved one of my lifelong dreams. I made the Olympic Team. I was going to represent the United States of America on the world's biggest stage.

Finally, it was over. It was a little bit of a nightmare that I finally woke up from. Anxiety was replaced with eagerness.

It was a wild, crazy and chaotic summer. It didn't fully set in that I was an Olympian for a while. It didn't really set in until I arrived in Sydney, Australia for the 2000 Olympic Games.

## CHAPTER 7
# EXPERIENCE OF A LIFETIME

It was a long journey filled with twists and turns. And highs and lows. But I had finally made my first U.S. Olympic Team at age 30.

Most athletes are already done competing by that point in their lives, but I knew that this was what I supposed to be doing. This was where God gifted and placed me. I wasn't ready to stop competing, regardless of what my results were. I had complete faith in what I was doing.

And even with many of the setbacks and heartbreak that I had endured, it was a journey I still enjoyed and embraced.

What I was able to do sends a message of perseverance. I wrestled on the Senior level for a lot of years against some of the best wrestlers on the planet. I made an abundance of sacrifices to reach that level. And stay there. It took me a long time before I became the No. 1 guy at my weight class in the United States.

With the protests and the case going to arbitration after the 2000 Olympic Trials, my family didn't have much time to plan for the trip to Sydney, Australia for the Olympic Games.

But it was still an exciting time for my family. And a handful of them were planning to fly to Sydney and watch me compete. My wife, my father, my mother and stepdad, and my sister all traveled to the Olympics.

The United States Greco-Roman team arrived at the Olympics more than three weeks before the competition. We

## NOT ALL ROADS LEAD TO GOLD

arrived in Australia at the end of August. Our competition was scheduled for September 26 and 27.

Arriving early gave us plenty of time to acclimate and gave us a few weeks to finish our final training cycle before the tournament. And it also gave us a chance to take part in the Opening Ceremonies and take in the full Olympic experience.

Following the Olympic Trials in June, the American Greco team had mostly practiced at the U.S. Olympic Training Center in Colorado Springs.

When we arrived in Australia, we trained at a facility just a few hours outside Sydney. We spent a majority of our time there leading up to the competition.

We then moved to the Olympic Village with all of the other athletes a few days before the Olympic Games started.

We didn't have much time to watch other sports, but I attended a soccer match at the Olympics before we competed. A few guys on our wrestling team went to watch.

Sydney was an excellent choice as a host city for the Olympics. It's an amazing place. It is a beautiful and scenic city, and the people were extremely friendly. I've been all over the world, and it's one of the best cities I've ever visited. I loved going there and I'm looking forward to going back again someday.

The best part, by far, of my pre-competition experience was the Opening Ceremonies. It was an incredible experience. And it was held far enough before our competition that it didn't interrupt any of our training. Everybody on our team went and they were not disappointed.

The folks from the U.S. Olympic Committee had given us an idea of what to expect in Sydney. And it was no secret that attending the Opening Ceremonies required a huge time commitment.

The athletes gathered several hours ahead of time at the Olympic Village and then took a bus to the Olympic Stadium.

We had to sit around for several hours before athletes from each country entered the stadium near the end of the night. It was

## *A path of persistence, faith and perseverance*

an extremely long evening, but it was more than worth it.

It was amazing having an opportunity to walk into a sold-out stadium with 100,000 enthusiastic fans cheering us on. It was awesome. And then thinking that a gazillion people are watching on TV, that is pretty special. The Olympics are the biggest sporting event on the planet. And I was very honored, blessed and humbled to be able to take part in it.

It was a huge adrenaline rush to walk into that stadium for the Opening Ceremonies. It was an experience I will never forget. I'm usually someone who doesn't become starstruck if I see a celebrity or a famous athlete. But this was different. It was definitely interesting when I saw a young athlete who everyone was talking about.

I stood next to basketball player Yao Ming of China. He was two feet taller than me and outweighed me by 160 pounds. He stood 7-foot-5 and weighed 300 pounds. I was 5-5 and 140 pounds. He was the tallest person I had ever seen in my life. He was just 20 years old and people were fascinated by seeing a human being that size. Yao was smiling and seemed like he was having a great time. Everybody wanted to say hello to him.

It also was interesting to see wrestlers from other countries, including many I recognized, taking part in the Opening Ceremonies. And I witnessed first-hand how important an event this was and see the enormous pride athletes took in representing their countries.

I know I was incredibly honored to be representing the United States of America on the world's biggest stage. I was very focused on my training and preparation for my competition, but I also took time to enjoy that evening and soak it all in. It was quite a night.

I also met American track and field sprinter Maurice Greene, who went on to win two Olympic gold medals in Sydney.

Walking into the stadium with all of the other U.S. athletes, you really do feel a huge sense of pride for your country. I definitely was fortunate to be a part of such a rare opportunity.

It was very late when we rode buses back to the Olympic

## NOT ALL ROADS LEAD TO GOLD

Village following the Opening Ceremonies. When I finally made it back to my room, I was exhausted. But it was an amazing experience.

Being an Olympian had been my dream for many years and now it had finally become a reality. I felt great when I went to bed that night, but that feeling didn't last long. I woke up a few hours later and I was in excruciating pain.

I woke up with a terrible toothache. The next morning, I talked to one of our coaches, Dan Chandler, and he sent me to the dentist. I resisted at first because I didn't want to miss a workout. Dan insisted I see the dentist and it's a good thing that he did. My tooth had abscessed. I cracked one of my fillings a few years before while wrestling against Ivan Ivanov during a practice in 1997. I didn't have my tooth fixed at the time because I didn't have the money to pay for it.

My tooth had become infected at the Olympics. The timing wasn't the best obviously, but it was better than having it happen the morning that I competed.

I ended up having a partial root canal eight days before I was supposed to compete. Instead of resting like I should have, I grabbed one of our training partners, Chris Saba, and tried to sweat it out of my system by working out. It was an unwise decision – I needed to rest and recover. I was feeling better by the time I competed, but I felt like I was a little bit off after that had become an issue.

I still wasn't feeling 100 percent on September 25, 2000, when I made weight for the Olympics at 58 kilograms. The Greco-Roman competition at the Olympics would be held the following two days on September 26 and 27.

The brackets were drawn immediately after weigh-ins, but some wrestlers choose not to look at their draw until the following morning. I was one of those people who didn't want to know who I was wrestling until the next day. I just wanted to refuel, recover and rest after weighing in. I didn't want to have to worry about who I was going to wrestle. I remember Saba walking up to me shortly after weigh-ins.

## *A path of persistence, faith and perseverance*

"I saw your bracket," he said. "And I like your draw."

I just nodded at him and didn't say anything. I still wanted to wait until the next morning before I saw who I was going to wrestle.

In a lot of ways, the Olympics were like any other tournament for me. I followed the same routine I always did. I rehydrated and ate dinner to refuel my body after weigh-ins before heading to bed.

I had to be super disciplined with my diet to make 58 kilograms. That translated to around 128 pounds. My natural weight during that time was around 140. And I was a lean 140, so there wasn't much to cut when I dropped down to my competition weight.

Luckily, I had my weight under control and had managed it well. And I was feeling good after having dinner that evening.

Fortunately, I was able to shut my brain off and fall asleep shortly after my head hit the pillow. I was able to get a good night's sleep and I felt rested when I woke up the morning of competition.

I was still just a little bit off from the root canal and it had taken something out of me. I didn't feel quite as powerful. Or as energetic. There was nothing I could do about it. I just had to battle through it and compete as hard as I could.

I continued to try and follow the same routine I had for any other tournament. I woke up and ate breakfast before heading over to the arena.

But reality quickly set in that morning. This wasn't just any other tournament. This was the Olympic Games. And these were going to be the biggest matches of my life. I had trained for years and traveled all around the world to have this opportunity.

Shortly after arriving at the venue, we found the warmup area. I laced up my shoes and began jogging around the perimeter of the mats.

After doing some stretching and some warmup drills, I grabbed teammate Kevin Bracken and we started wrestling. I hit an assortment of techniques, throws and holds at a fast pace while

## NOT ALL ROADS LEAD TO GOLD

elevating my heart rate. I finished with a hard two-minute push to prepare for my first match.

Beads of sweat trickled down my face as I made my final preparations. My blood was pumping and my adrenaline was flowing. I was ready to go.

I really did try to treat it like any other tournament to calm my nerves and keep my composure. But it was still the Olympics, and the arena was packed with fans. It was still a little intimidating.

Earlier that morning, shortly after I woke up, I finally looked at my bracket. There were 20 wrestlers in the 58-kilogram bracket and it was divided into six pools of wrestlers.

I was drawn into a three-man pool with wrestlers from Armenia and Belarus. The winner of the pool would advance to the quarterfinal round. My initial thoughts were that I liked my draw. I had dominated the Armenian, Karen Mnatsakanyan, in February at the Olympic qualifier in France. I beat him handily, winning by technical superiority.

That gave me a good feeling going into my first match at the Olympics. I knew it was a winnable match against the Armenian.

I had tried to keep all of my preparations for the Olympics business-like. I did everything in my power to eliminate as many distractions as I could. And I did that for the most part.

At 30 years old, I was a veteran with an abundance of international experience on the Senior level. But I also was a first-time Olympian who was wrestling on the sport's biggest stage for the first time.

Even with so much at stake, I was confident when I walked into the arena for my first match. U.S. National Coach Steve Fraser was in my corner.

And my name was announced over the loudspeakers.

"Now wrestling, from the United States of America, Jim Gruenwald."

I slapped hands with my coaches and jogged to the center of the mat. It was time. I shook hands with my opponent and the whistle blew to start the match. And I quickly realized this would

## A path of persistence, faith and perseverance

be a much different match from the one we wrestled in February. It was going to be much more difficult.

The Armenian was ready to battle. My Olympic debut was a knock-down, drag-out backyard brawl. This was the Olympic Games and this match was going to be a dogfight. It was a fierce bout against a strong, physical and determined opponent.

I wanted to set a fast pace and I charged out aggressively. I eventually struck first in the match and took control. I scored a takedown and followed by turning him with a gut-wrench for two points. I was up 3-0.

But there was no quit in the Armenian. Down by three, he stormed right back. The whistle blew and I was put in the down position for passivity late in the second period. He took advantage of his opportunity, turning me with a gut wrench to draw within 3-2. Then he scored a lift to tie the match 3-3.

His corner was going crazy – his coaches were jumping up and down after he had tied the match.

Just when it looked like he was going to send the match into overtime, I dug down deep in the final seconds. I broke free for an escape and hit a duck under to spin behind him for a takedown with less than a second left.

I completed the takedown just an eyelash before 6:00 flashed on the scoreboard to signify the end of the six-minute bout. Now my coaches were jumping up and down in celebration.

The referees reviewed video of the final sequence and confirmed that I had scored the takedown. That was a huge relief.

I didn't really celebrate. I was too tired to do much of anything. I was down on one knee, trying to catch my breath during the video review. I was exhausted. Welcome to the Olympic Games.

It turned out that the Armenian I defeated was very tough. He went on to win a silver medal the following year at the World Championships.

I had won my Olympic debut, but I had to quickly turn my focus to my next match. I would battle Igor Petrenko of Belarus. I needed to defeat him to win my pool and advance to the

## NOT ALL ROADS LEAD TO GOLD

quarterfinals.

I knew it was going to be a challenge. Petrenko had taken fourth at the 1999 World Championships. And he had beaten Dennis Hall in that tournament.

It also was Petrenko's second straight trip to the Olympics. He was a seasoned veteran. It would be the first time I had wrestled him.

I came out aggressively again and grabbed the early lead. I scored a one-point takedown and hit a gut-wrench turn for two points. I added a late takedown with a slide-by – I elevated an underhook on the left side and eventually dropped down to go behind him for a point.

I won the match decisively, earning a 4-0 victory while shutting him down. It was a huge win for me against an excellent wrestler.

Following all of the controversy with Dennis Hall after the Olympic Trials, that was a big win for me because Petrenko had beaten Dennis the year before. The win over Petrenko validated my win over Dennis and gave me credibility.

I had won my pool and had advanced to the quarterfinals of the Olympics. It was super exciting to win that match. I had clinched a top-six finish at the Olympic Games.

I was done for the day and would return to compete the next morning in the quarterfinals. I went out and ate dinner with my family before going back to the Olympic Village to relax.

I came back on Day 2 for my quarterfinal bout against another tough opponent: Sheng Zetian of China. Sheng was a veteran who had won Olympic bronze medals in 1992 and 1996. He also had been a World silver medalist in 1998.

He was an experienced wrestler with a sparkling resume. I had not wrestled him, but I still came in confident in my chances. I had come a long way to reach this point and I wasn't backing down from anybody. I didn't care how impressive his resume was. I was there to win.

The match with Sheng was a hard-fought, low-scoring affair for the first four minutes. I scored a one-point lift and took a 1-0

## *A path of persistence, faith and perseverance*

lead in the first period.

The start of the second period was uneventful, but with two minutes remaining I imploded. I was put down by the officials for passivity and Sheng capitalized. He lifted me and threw me for like a thousand points – or at least it seemed that way.

When he launched me, he was awarded four points for the throw and one point for a high amplitude move. He also was given two points after they called a leg foul on me. All of a sudden, I was in big trouble. I was down 7-1.

Just when it looked like it couldn't get any worse, it did. The officials put me right back in the down position again. He lifted me and gutted me to end the match. I lost the match 11-1.

I went from a 1-0 lead with two minutes left in the bout to him scoring a ton of points in the blink of an eye. He had defeated me by technical superiority after building a 10-point lead. I didn't even make it to the end of the six-minute match. It was awful. It was stunning. And it was like a punch in the gut.

I came to Sydney to win a gold medal. I was winning my quarterfinal match and then everything goes sideways. And I get crushed. It was horrible. My medal hopes were over. The best I could finish now was fifth place.

Sheng went on to win his third straight Olympic bronze medal. My setback to Sheng had dropped me down into the fifth-place match.

I'm normally pretty good at hitting the reset button, but this was different. It was the Olympics and I had just suffered a tough setback. And I no longer had a chance to reach the medal podium.

But I had a chance to feel a little bit better if I could win my next match. Finally, I tried to regroup. I kept telling myself that fifth place was still better than sixth.

I came back and wrestled hard before falling to Iran's Ali Ashkani in the fifth-place match. The Iranian was tough, as I expected. Everybody who wrestles in the Olympics is typically a hammer.

He had a good set of lungs and I wasn't able to wear him down like I had hoped. I made a huge mistake against the Iranian.

## NOT ALL ROADS LEAD TO GOLD

I was trying to turn him, but he countered my gut-wrench attempt and stepped over me. And then he lifted me. He won the match 3-2. It was a disappointing finish. I had such high hopes after winning my first two matches.

It's such an emotional roller coaster when you compete at the Olympics. I tried to treat it like any other tournament so I could keep my focus, but it's a huge event with so much on the line.

To lose a match at that level, most people can't fathom what that feels like. It's brutal. It's heartbreaking. And it stings.

The Olympics happen just once every four years and the event carries such huge importance. It's so rare to even have an opportunity to compete on that stage.

It was quite a journey just making it to the 2000 Olympics Games. It took an unbelievable amount of work for the United States just to qualify my weight class for the Olympics.

And then I had to beat a World champion and Olympic silver medalist in Dennis Hall just to make the American team. Then I had to go through the process where he protested the loss to me in the Olympic Trials and then took it to arbitration.

It was a long, grueling and stressful year, but it was more than worth it when I stepped on the mat in Sydney, Australia. I had reached my goal of becoming an Olympian. And I received an opportunity to compete on the biggest stage in our sport.

Even though I didn't reach my ultimate goal, it was still amazing to represent my country in Sydney. It was the experience of a lifetime and I eventually realized how thankful I should be for the opportunity.

The good news was this wasn't the end. I knew I wasn't done. I felt like my career was just starting. I just made my first U.S. team on the Senior level. Why would I stop now?

Being a math teacher, I broke down just how difficult it was for an athlete to even reach the Olympic Games. To make an Olympic Team as a wrestler, you have a .001 percent chance to make it in the United States.

For all of the people who compete in wrestling at any stage of their lives, those are the odds that you have of making an

## A path of persistence, faith and perseverance

Olympic Team. I knew it was a significant achievement for me to become an Olympian.

But it still hurt when I lost because I knew how close I was to winning a medal. I was able to take solace in the fact that I wasn't done wrestling. I was ready to commit to another four-year Olympic cycle through 2004. I would be back.

Before that, I reflected on my experience and put it into perspective. Our successes and failures, they don't define you. They direct you. You learn from the experience and you move on with your life. If you don't, your life is going to be even more challenging.

I was done wrestling at the 2000 Olympics, but Team USA still had one final opportunity for glory in Sydney. After I had lost in my fifth-place match, we came back that evening for the medal matches.

American heavyweight Rulon Gardner had advanced to the Greco-Roman finals against three-time Olympic gold medalist Alexander Karelin of Russia.

The pudgy, boyish-looking Gardner grew up on a dairy farm in Wyoming and he was a huge underdog going into the finals.

The 6-foot-3 Karelin, a powerful wrestler with a chiseled physique, had also won nine World titles. He hadn't lost an international wrestling match in 13 years and was considered one of the greatest wrestlers of all-time.

Sitting in the stands that night, I gave Rulon zero chance of beating Karelin. None. I had watched Karelin smash Rulon and almost kill him when they had wrestled a few years before in a tournament in Russia. Karelin folded Rulon in half and almost broke his back in the previous match they had. Those guys were on different levels.

Even before the match, people were already praising Karelin for becoming the first wrestler to win four Olympic gold medals in wrestling.

An announcement actually came over the loudspeakers after the semifinals. The announcer said to "Come back tonight for Alexander Karelin's 13th gold medal ceremony."

## NOT ALL ROADS LEAD TO GOLD

A win over Rulon would have given him a total of 13 gold medals with four Olympic titles and nine World titles. The ceremony was a foregone conclusion. In most people's eyes anyway. Including mine.

There was no way Karelin was going to lose. Especially not to a relatively unknown wrestler like Rulon Gardner.

I was sitting with my teammates when the match started. Everybody in the arena thought Rulon was going to lose, including me and my teammates. We obviously wanted Ru to win, but so much was stacked against him. Karelin was just too good and he was going to cap his legendary career with one final title.

Everyone expected Rulon Gardner to lose – except Rulon and the American coaches. Our coaches had put together a masterful game plan and Rulon followed it as closely as he possibly could. Rulon stuck to the plan and kept the match scoreless.

The match was still 0-0 when they went to overtime. Karelin broke his lock in the clinch and Rulon was awarded a point. After he scored the point in the clinch, I knew Rulon had a chance to do it. He had a chance to knock off a legend.

Rulon still led 1-0 as the final seconds ticked off the clock. Karelin was unable to rally. The match ended. And it was pandemonium.

An unknown American named Rulon Gardner had upset Russian legend Alexander Karelin in the finals of the 2000 Olympic Games.

Announcer Russ Hellickson summed it up perfectly on the NBC broadcast.

"Do you believe in miracles again?" Hellickson said excitedly as the match ended.

Gardner celebrated with a cartwheel after earning his shocking victory. It was one of the biggest upsets in Olympic history. In any sport. It was crazy. We were super excited. We were jumping up and down, and high-fiving. How could you not be excited? How did this just happen?

## A path of persistence, faith and perseverance

I was Rulon's teammate and had roomed with him on numerous overseas trips. I trained alongside the guy for several years, but I didn't see this coming.

Before the match, I didn't think it was possible. But that's the beauty of athletics. You just never know sometimes what's going to happen.

That win did a lot for Greco-Roman wrestling at the time. It brought a lot of attention to the sport. It shows you on any given day, anybody can beat anybody at that level.

Everybody loves an underdog and it was a heck of a story when Rulon won. It was an unbelievable accomplishment for him. I was extremely happy for Rulon. I was excited for him, but I also was disappointed because I thought I could win a gold medal of my own.

We stuck around and watched Rulon's gold medal ceremony. I stood with my hand over my heart as the Star-Spangled Banner was played in the arena and the red, white and blue American flag was raised.

Karelin was in a place he had never been before, standing on the step below Rulon on the podium with a silver medal hanging around his neck. It was a historic and magical night. It was almost unthinkable what had just happened. It was a great night to be an American.

That match definitely inspired me and motivated me. I knew that if Rulon could do it, I could do it. That gave me a boost at the end of a tough day for me personally after I fell short of my goals.

It was bittersweet for me. I was super excited for my teammate and I knew I was very close to doing the same thing.

Our Olympic journey in 2000 did end with another memorable experience. All of the American athletes that took part in the Olympics were invited to the White House shortly after returning home from Australia.

I traveled to the White House with my Greco-Roman teammates. I had an opportunity to shake hands with President Bill Clinton. It was exciting with all of the U.S. Olympians being there.

## NOT ALL ROADS LEAD TO GOLD

We went in one-by-one to meet the President and shake his hand. It was kind of surreal. When I shook his hand, I said, "Thank you for having us." He smiled and said, "Thank you!"
After we all shook hands with him, President Clinton gave a speech and we took a big group photo with him.

Going to the White House was a great experience. It was a historical place that I had always wanted to see. It was awesome to be there and have a chance to interact briefly with the President.

As the year 2000 drew to a close, I was ready to embark on my next journey. My quest to make the next Olympic Team in 2004. I knew it wasn't going to be easy, but I was ready to pursue my next challenge.

## CHAPTER 8
# OLYMPIC QUEST, PART II

My quest for a second straight Olympic berth began with the start of the new four-year Olympic cycle in 2001.

I had finally overcome one of my biggest obstacles in defeating Dennis Hall to make the 2000 Olympic Team. I had reached the quarterfinals of the Olympic Games and earned a top-six finish.

I was feeling optimistic and positive going into the following season. Now I had my sights set squarely on another goal. Making my first World Team.

I had a good winter tour season in 2001. I won the Hungarian Grand Prix and finished third in a tough tournament in Greece. I also won a silver medal at the Pan American Championships. I had continued to wrestle well following the Olympics.

I had knocked off Dennis Hall, but he wasn't going anywhere. We met again in the finals of the 2001 U.S. Open at 58 kg and he was ready for me.

It was no secret that Dennis was still upset about losing to me in 2000 and he defeated me by a 5-0 decision in the 2001 U.S. Open finals. I had finished second in the U.S. Open for the sixth consecutive season.

Being the great competitor that he was, Dennis was determined to bounce back. And he did. It was a super intense

## NOT ALL ROADS LEAD TO GOLD

match. At one point, I ran him out of bounds and gave him a little shove. And then I smiled at him. He glared at me and made a comment.

"I'm not afraid of you," he said.

Dennis wrestled well, but I knew I would receive another shot at him that summer at the World Team Trials in Cincinnati, Ohio.

That loss to Dennis didn't deflate me. It just fired me up and gave me more motivation. I had been wrestling at a high level internationally and that gave me confidence.

I advanced to the finals of the Trials to meet Dennis, who was sitting out after winning the Open.

We had two hard-fought matches at the Trials, and I won both bouts in overtime, 3-0 and 3-0. We were put in the clinch in both matches and I was able to score both times.

We ended up in this weird scramble. His head was there and I just grabbed it and yanked him backward. His back exposed to the mat and I scored two points.

It may not have been pretty, but I beat Dennis in two straight matches. And that's all that mattered. That was the first time I had won two straight matches against Dennis Hall in a Trials.

It was more validation after what happened in 2000 with the protests and my Olympic Trials win over him going to arbitration.

I had beaten Dennis two years in a row to make a U.S. Team. And at the age of 31 years old, I had finally made my first U.S. World Team.

Those matches with Dennis were so emotional and so draining. I obviously was elated that I won, but I had burned so much energy to do it.

Part of that was my age. I was still in peak physical condition. But I was also 31, and I was at an age where a lot of people are done wrestling.

I was at a point in my career where I wasn't going to be jumping around and clapping my hands when I won a big match. I expected to be there and I had been there before after making the Olympic Team.

## *A path of persistence, faith and perseverance*

I had asked Mike Houck to be in my corner in Cincinnati. Mike was the first American to win a World title in Greco-Roman wrestling and he had been the U.S. National Coach.

Mike had coached me at the Olympic Training Center for three years. He had drifted from the sport for a few years so it was great having him back in my corner and having his support at the Trials. It meant a lot to me. By that time, our relationship had gone from coach-athlete to coach-friend, and I remember him thanking me for the opportunity.

Those wins over Dennis Hall landed me a spot in the 2001 World Championships. The World Championships were scheduled for late September at Madison Square Garden in New York City.

I was training to compete in my home country. I had finally made it to my first World Championships and it was going to be held in the United States.

I was excited to have the opportunity to compete in front of our American fans in one of the world's most famous arenas.

It was going to be a marquee event for wrestling and provide unprecedented exposure for our sport in one of the world's biggest cities.

We were in the final stages of our training for the World Championships when the awful news broke. I walked into practice on the morning of September 11, 2001, and heard the devastating news. Our coaches informed us there had been terrorist attacks that occurred in New York City and Washington, D.C.

Four American planes had been hijacked by terrorists. Terrorists crashed two planes into the World Trade Center Towers in New York. Another plane had hit the Pentagon in Washington and a fourth plane crashed in a field in Pennsylvania.

Nearly 3,000 people were killed during the 9/11 terrorist attacks. Everything changed that day when those innocent people lost their lives in those horrific attacks.

It was a terrible situation. It was unbelievable and difficult to comprehend that something this tragic had happened in our

## NOT ALL ROADS LEAD TO GOLD

country. We were in shock. And our practices were cancelled that day.

A number of major sporting events were postponed and rescheduled in the wake of the tragedy. And the World Championships followed suit. FILA, wrestling's international governing body, decided to postpone the Worlds. They also decided to change the venue and not hold the event in New York City.

It obviously was the right thing to do after the tragedy. It definitely put what we did as Olympic-level athletes in perspective.

Lives had been lost in a senseless and unspeakable tragedy. And the entire country was in mourning. And in a state of disbelief. My thoughts and prayers were with the families that were impacted by the attacks. I can't imagine what they were going through.

FILA eventually rescheduled the World Championships. And it was held more than two months later. The 2001 Greco-Roman World Championships were held in Patras, Greece in December.

I started strong. I won my first two matches to win my pool. I advanced to the quarterfinals and faced Iran's Ali Ashkani, the wrestler I had lost to in the fifth-place match the year before at the Olympics.

I made another mistake in the rematch and it cost me again. I lost the match. I finished 10th at my first World Championships. I didn't wrestle as well as I should have. And that was disappointing.

Having the tournament moved from the U.S. to Greece definitely had a negative impact on me. We missed out on the opportunity to wrestle at home and it just wasn't the same wrestling halfway around the world. But at the same time, I was an experienced wrestler who had competed extensively overseas.

I had to once again hit the reset button and keep moving forward. I had made my first World Team and continued to gain momentum for the next Olympics. And I had now gained

## *A path of persistence, faith and perseverance*

valuable experience from competing at a World Championships.

In 2002, FILA reduced the number of Greco-Roman weight classes from eight to seven. It was tough to see us lose another weight class. Greco had previously had 10 divisions before it was cut to eight. Now we were down to seven.

The one good part about the change was that I did like the new weight classes. I was able to move up two kilograms to the new division of 60 kilograms/132 pounds. I didn't have to cut as much weight. I was moving up 4.4 pounds and I felt stronger in the new division. I had another good winter tour season, placing second in big tournaments in Bulgaria and Greece.

In my first important domestic competition at my new weight class, I teched my way to the finals and expected to face Hall for the billionth time. Then the unexpected happened. Glenn Nieradka had dropped down from 63 kg to 60 kg, and he beat Dennis.

I had beaten Nieradka pretty handily in two previous matches when I had moved up to 63 kg for smaller domestic competitions.

I wasn't overly concerned when Nieradka dropped to 60 kg for the U.S. Open, but his win over Hall obviously got my full attention.

Nieradka was exceptional in the clinch. He was a good thrower in the body lock position. But those were skills I could shut down with solid positioning by grinding him down.

Unfortunately, he shut down my offense and turned me with a gut-wrench to win 4-2. Losing to Nieradka was shocking. It was the first U.S. opponent other than Dennis Hall that I had lost to since 1996.

It was the seventh straight year I had placed second at the U.S. Open. If Twitter was around back then, I likely would have gone by the handle @alliseeissilver.

Nieradka had an amazing tournament and was named Outstanding Wrestler in Greco-Roman. With his win at the Open, Nieradka clinched a spot in the finals of June's World Team Trials in St. Paul, Minnesota.

## NOT ALL ROADS LEAD TO GOLD

To earn another shot at Nieradka, I would have to win the challenge tournament in St. Paul. And beat Dennis Hall again.

We were the top two seeds in the challenge tournament, and we advanced to the finals. I took control early before earning a 4-1 win over Dennis.

We obviously didn't know it at the time, but it would end up being the last time we would meet in competition.

We wrestled each other 23 times in our careers, dating back to high school. I finished with a 7-16 record against Dennis Hall.

I was winless against him over a 10-year period before I finally broke through. I eventually gained the upper hand late in our careers. I was 5-1 in the last six matches against him in U.S. Open or Team Trials competition.

Dennis obviously was a big part of my story and a huge part of my career. I sincerely believe he was a blessing from God and I'm thankful for the trailblazing he did for U.S. Greco-Roman wrestling.

Dennis had been the best wrestler in the World and he was a guy I was unable to defeat for a majority of my career. He is a Hall of Famer who is one of the best wrestlers in American Greco-Roman history.

Wrestling against Dennis Hall was one of the big reasons that I became successful on the international level. My quest to defeat him motivated me and drove me to be at my best.

He was a tremendous competitor who was one of the strongest and most physical wrestlers I ever faced. We had some incredible battles.

It is doubtful that Dennis and I will ever be the best of friends, but I love and respect the man. I know we pushed each other and made each other better. The dude is awesome.

Following that 2002 win over Dennis, I had to quickly shift my focus to a tough final-round series. I advanced to face Nieradka in the finals of the World Team Trials. He had been sitting while I battled Hall and others to win the challenge tournament.

Nieradka came out fresh and strong in the first match of our

## A path of persistence, faith and perseverance

best-of-3 finals series. He defeated me for the second straight time, scoring a 4-1 victory.

As I walked back into the warmup area, I was in a bit of a post-match rage. I was upset and let one of my coaches, Andy Seras, know about it.

"He will never beat me again," I told Seras.

I was in a familiar spot – down one match and needing to win the final two bouts to make the World Team. I battled back in Match No. 2 and earned a 3-0 victory. Now it would come down to the decisive third and final match.

I had been the top guy in the U.S. at my weight class the previous two years and I wasn't about to relinquish my No. 1 ranking. I earned a 4-0 win in the final match against Nieradka.

I needed to turn up the intensity and push the pace. I had a sense of urgency because I knew I couldn't lose another match to him. I told myself that the only thing greater than my will is God's will.

Everybody is looking for a reason to quit in a wrestling match and you have to be the one to give it to them. It goes back to the saying of "Fatigue makes cowards of us all."

My high level of conditioning was one of my greatest attributes. I focused a good part of my training on my muscular endurance, so I wouldn't wear down late in my matches.

Wrestling is neither a pure sprint or a marathon. It is like an 800-meter run and at times a mile. You are almost sprinting the whole time and at the same time you have someone trying to beat you up. That's what a wrestling match feels like. It's a grueling, excruciating battle of strength and stamina.

I survived the battle in Minnesota and I had made my second straight World Team. And I would hold the No. 1 national ranking for a third straight year after making the 2000 Olympic Team.

It obviously was the place where I wanted to be. But I still hadn't won a medal at the World Championships or the Olympics. And I was wrestling to serve God and win medals.

I headed to the 2002 World Championships in Moscow, Russia, with my sights set on winning a gold medal.

## NOT ALL ROADS LEAD TO GOLD

Before the tournament, I visualized how I would wrestle the tournament in different scenarios. In each scenario, I would end up winning the gold medal.

I was in a very tough weight class, but I had beaten a number of Olympic and World medalists in other international events. My confidence level was high.

I won my first two matches to capture my pool at the 2002 World Championships. I defeated Valentin Malutin of Kyrgyzstan 4-2 and followed by downing Seref Tufenk of Turkey 4-2. I was able to score a takedown and a gut wrench in each of those matches.

With those first two wins, I advanced to the quarterfinals against Greco legend Armen Nazaryan of Bulgaria. He had beaten me 5-0 earlier that season in the finals of a tournament in Bulgaria.

At that point, Nazaryan was a two-time Olympic champion. And he was at his peak as a wrestler.

I knew it was going to take an incredible performance to beat him. I knew he had a great reverse lift and I felt like if I got on top that I could turn him.

We started the match on our feet and I was put down for passivity. Nazaryan only needed one time on top. He locked up a reverse lift and started piling up the points.

He threw me like 20 times, but the referees only saw two or three, and that's all they needed to see. I think he scored about a thousand points, but he ended up with a 10-0 win by technical superiority. I didn't even make it out of the first period.

To say I was frustrated and embarrassed is a gross understatement. I went from losing 5-0 to him in his home country to getting crushed 10-0 at the World Championships. It was awful – just awful.

He was so powerful and so good with his reverse lift. Once he locked that up, you were in big trouble. I knew I needed to learn how to better defend against him.

I had no chance to wrestle back after losing to Nazaryan and I finished in eighth place. Nazaryan went on to win the World

## A path of persistence, faith and perseverance

title.

Ultimately, it was my fault. When I was put down in par terre, I wasn't prepared. There was a lot of work to do as I continued to gain experience as we moved closer to the 2004 Olympics.

I entered the 2003 season as an Olympian and a two-time World Team member, but there was still one goal I had never achieved.

I had never won the U.S. Open, but I knew I had a strong chance to change that. I rolled into the finals for the eighth straight year.

We had a break before the finals and I grabbed something to eat. On the way back to the Las Vegas Convention Center, I was riding in a car with close friend Ethan Bosch when an advertisement on one of the marquees caught my eye. It was for an REO Speedwagon and Styx concert that evening.

I turned to Bosch and said: "I might as well just go to that concert. I've lost seven years in a row – everyone knows what is going to happen. Let's just go to that show instead."

All joking aside, I was ready to wrestle. After seven straight years of setbacks in the U.S. Open finals, I was ready for a reversal of fortune.

My luck finally changed that night. I took command early before defeating Glenn Nieradka 6-0 in the finals. After seven straight second-place finishes, I was finally a U.S. Open champion.

A short time after I came off the mat, I saw my brother-in-law and my sister-in-law. They had come to Las Vegas to watch me compete. When we first started talking, my sister-in-law made a comment.

"That didn't look so hard," she said.

I had to laugh. I had been in the same exact position seven years before and had lost every time. Now I had finally broken through.

I was named Outstanding Wrestler of the tournament. It was a relief, but it was also exciting because I had finally won a

## NOT ALL ROADS LEAD TO GOLD

national title.

I had captured my first USA Wrestling stop-sign plaque on the Senior level. And I wouldn't have to give it back this time like I did in 1996. I carried the momentum from the U.S. Open into the rest of the season.

I swept Nieradka in the finals of the 2003 World Team Trials in Indianapolis. I won the first match 4-0 before prevailing 3-1 in overtime in the second match.

In the first bout, I scored with a three-point throw. In the second bout, we were tied 1-1 in OT before I scored a takedown and gut-wrench to win. I had made my third straight World Team and now was the time to go win a medal.

The 2003 World Championships would be held in Creteil, France. The event carried added significance because it also was the first qualifier for the 2004 Olympic Games. The top six qualifiers in each weight class would qualify their countries for the Olympics.

I came out strong by downing World silver medalist Karen Mnatsakanyan of Armenia by a 6-3 score in overtime. I had already beaten him a couple of times, but he had improved. It was a crazy match. He was winning 3-0, but I battled back. I hit a duck under, he countered and I hit a headlock to tie the match.

We got in a scramble in overtime and I hit a hip toss for three points to win the match. The guy was like 10 feet tall and he was difficult to wrestle against. He was the skinniest, tallest guy I ever wrestled. It was ridiculous. He was very thin, but he also was very strong.

I ended up losing my second match, falling to Hungary's Laszlo Bona 4-1. I tried to gut-wrench him, but he stepped over me for a reversal. He then turned me and was ahead 4-0. I was trying to score late in the match and then he was called for fleeing the mat. I scored a point. I had beaten Bona twice before, but it didn't happen this time.

In the first match in our pool, Mnatsakanyan beat Bona. All three of us finished 1-1 in the pool, but I won the pool with the most classification points.

## *A path of persistence, faith and perseverance*

I won the pool by virtue of scoring the one point in the match I lost. Pushing hard to the end and scoring that point was the only way I advanced. It's hard to explain and comprehend the rules sometimes, but the good news was that I was headed to the quarterfinals.

I advanced to the quarterfinal round to face Egypt's Ashraf Mohamed, a Junior World silver medalist who ended up making three Olympic teams.

I took control in the quarters and earned a 5-0 victory over Ashraf. I was able to take him down and turn him with a gut-wrench after he was called for passivity. That victory carried huge significance for me and my country.

I had advanced to the semifinals and clinched a top-four finish. And I had qualified the U.S. for the 2004 Olympic Games at my weight class.

My reward for reaching the semifinals? Another match against two-time Olympic champion and reigning World champion Armen Nazaryan of Bulgaria.

In two meetings the previous season, he had beaten me by a combined 15-0 margin.

But I had another chance to face Nazaryan again before the 2003 World Championships. We met in the Kurt Angle Classic and he barely beat me in overtime. I knew the gap had closed with the work I had done to defend his reverse lift. I knew I could compete with him.

I had been training for another shot at the Greco legend and this was my opportunity. I was one win away from reaching the gold-medal match.

The match with Nazaryan was exciting. I was down 1-0 and I was put down for passivity, but I was able to reverse him. Now I felt like I had the momentum.

There was a minute left and I was pushing Nazaryan all over the mat. I knew I was about to take control of the bout. And then disaster struck.

He started his signature move and went to lift me before I tried to counter him. Nazaryan threw me and I tried to post my

## NOT ALL ROADS LEAD TO GOLD

arm on the mat as he brought me down. I landed awkwardly on the mat and dislocated my left shoulder.

I didn't realize how severe the injury was at first, but after a few seconds I was in excruciating pain. My shoulder had dislocated. I was in bad shape, but I wasn't going to stop wrestling.

I was in the semifinals of the World Championships. There was no way I could quit now. U.S. National Coach Steve Fraser approached me and reality finally set in.

"Jim, I'm calling it," he said.

I slowly nodded my head while holding my arm in agony. It was the first time in my life that I didn't finish a match.

I started crying. It was awful. And I was in tremendous pain. I felt like I was on the verge of beating one of the best pound-for-pound Greco wrestlers of all-time.

I walked back to the warmup area and our doctors were trying to relocate my shoulder, but it refused to move.

While still on the mat, the French doctor didn't realize my shoulder had dislocated. He was trying to rotate the arm to get a fix on the problem. I was yelling and he was asking me to calm down, which made me want to punch him. The muscles became immovable. Eventually, they allowed the American doctor on the mat, who had seen the injury in real time and knew what to do.

After a few unsuccessful attempts, the American doctor, John Pak, told me I had to relax, or they would have to take me to a hospital and put me out. The Cuban heavyweight was watching and offered to help. Dr. Pak bent my arm at the elbow, wrapped a towel around my forearm and gave an end to the Cuban and the other to our athletic trainer, Rod Rodriguez. They pulled, I screamed and Dr. Pak guided my shoulder back into place.

We talked briefly about the idea of me going back out to wrestle in the bronze-medal match. But the doctor said if I wrestled in that match there was a 99.9 percent chance it would dislocate again.

My wife even walked back into the warmup arena.

## *A path of persistence, faith and perseverance*

"You're an idiot if you even think about wrestling," she said.

"I'm an idiot because I already thought about it," I said back to her in frustration.

We made the decision fairly quickly. I wasn't going to wrestle. I had to default to the Romanian, Eusebiu Diaconu, in the bronze-medal match. He was a guy I had beaten 3-2 in Bulgaria in 2002.

It was one of the worst moments of my career. On every level. Physically, emotionally and spiritually. I remember shaking my fist at God and thinking how could this happen to me. I had done everything right. I had eaten right, trained right, listened to my coaches and lived the type of lifestyle I needed to be successful.

I was in a bad place. Character isn't built in the tough moments, it's revealed. I repented and asked for forgiveness from God after being upset with what had happened. And I eventually hit the reset button.

I had placed fourth at the World Championships. I had just missed the medal podium after not having the chance to wrestle back for bronze. I was improving on the World stage and my trajectory was good.

The following week, I had surgery after I returned home to Colorado Springs. The injury was even more severe than we initially thought. I had a 270-degree tear of my labrum and a partial tear of my biceps tendon. And I tore the glenohumeral ligament off the bone.

Dr. John Pak put five titanium screws into my shoulder to hold everything together. After the surgery, Dr. Pak sat down with me and talked to me about my road back.

"Your recovery will be about a year," he said.

That was not the news I wanted to hear.

"No, no, no," I responded while shaking my head. "I can't sit out that long. The Olympics are coming up."

It was early October and I was hoping to be back on the mat by April for the U.S. Open.

"Jim, I'm not clearing you to wrestle that soon," Dr. Pak

## NOT ALL ROADS LEAD TO GOLD

said.

But I was determined to make it back. I was in a sling for six weeks after the surgery. With the Olympics right around the corner, there was no way I could sit out a year. In my mind, I didn't have a choice. I was the No. 1 guy and had just qualified the weight class for the Olympics. I wasn't ready to be done. And I knew I had to make a run at the 2004 Olympics.

I was named USA Wrestling Greco-Roman Wrestler of the Year in 2003. It had been the best year of my career. I had finished fourth at the World Championships and had qualified the U.S. for the Olympics at 60 kilograms.

I also earned around $20,000 in 2003 with prize money, stipends and bonuses for my performances. I had been so close to achieving my dreams.

The good news was I still had an opportunity to reach my goals as we moved closer to the 2004 Olympic Games.

I had plenty of work to do while recovering from a horrible injury. But I was determined to make it back. Nothing was going to stop me.

## CHAPTER 9
# RETURN TO THE OLYMPICS

Following my shoulder surgery, my arm was in a sling for six weeks. I couldn't even lift my left arm when the sling came off. That's how severe my injury was.

Dr. Pak, my orthopedic surgeon, told me I wouldn't be able to wrestle for a year. But there was no way that could happen. I wasn't going to miss out on an opportunity to make my second straight U.S. Olympic Team. Especially after being the No. 1 guy at my weight class for four consecutive years. I had worked too hard and achieved too much in that Olympic cycle to miss out on this opportunity.

I started my rehabilitation with a goal of making it back for April's U.S. Open. My surgery was in October and I couldn't do anything for six weeks after that.

It was one of the most difficult times of my wrestling career, but I was motivated by the idea of beating the odds and qualifying for the Olympics.

I started my rehab, and as expected, it was a long, challenging and grueling process. I had a huge sense of urgency because I only had 4½ months to prepare for the U.S. Open.

I had already qualified for June's Olympic Trials in Indianapolis, but I wanted to make it back in time for the U.S. Open.

It was important to wrestle in the Open because I would go in as the No. 1 seed. And if I won the tournament, I would earn a

## NOT ALL ROADS LEAD TO GOLD

berth into the finals of the Olympic Trials. In my mind, there was tremendous value for me to win the U.S. Open and position myself to win the Olympic Trials.

Once the sling came off, it was torture to get my arm to move. It would still be another three months before I was able to get back on the mat and actually wrestle again.

I was a workout fanatic, and missing out on some of the training drove me crazy. Not being able to do anything was difficult. And depressing at times.

I went from being able to do nearly 100 pullups without stopping to not even being able to reach up and grab the pullup bar.

I adopted the mindset of pushing the pace with my rehabilitation, but at the same time being smart about it. I respected the doctors, but I also knew my body and what I was capable of doing.

I did everything I could do to make it back. And I prayed hard. Everything had to fall into place for this to work. I had to attack my rehab as aggressively, yet wisely, as I could.

Tim Johnson, my good friend from the Fellowship of Christian Athletes and the voice of Big Ten wrestling, provided a great comment on my mindset.

"If you want to get Gruenwald to do something, tell him it's impossible and he can't."

Tim's statement couldn't have been more accurate. There may have been a bit of pride involved in my rehab as well. I was motivated and driven to make it back for the U.S. Open.

I wasn't able to wrestle live, so my focus was on strength and conditioning. I rode the exercise bike so much I could've entered the Tour de France that year. I worked hard on my cardiovascular endurance. I was able to start running again.

I was then able to start doing hand-fighting workouts on the mat. And I was eventually able to start doing pullups. I built myself up to where I could do 65 pullups without stopping.

The power I gained doing pullups really helped me in my road to recovery. My shoulder had become much stronger.

## A path of persistence, faith and perseverance

Pullups are great for strength and muscular endurance, but the single greatest tool at my disposal was the Upper Torso Ergometer (UBE) – the dreaded hand bike.

I wanted to rehab and prepare myself at the same time to compete at a high level. I pushed myself to the extreme to return, and the UBE was the refining fire. I have never been closer to throwing up in a workout than on the UBE. I would grab anyone who wanted to simulate a match. Most of my matches on the UBE were against Ethan Bosch, one of my closest friends but also four weights heavier than me at 84 kg. His size gave him the advantage, and I needed the strain of overwhelming odds.

The week before the U.S. Open, I went to see Dr. Pak. He told me nearly six months before that I would be out for a year after he performed surgery on me.

But my rehab had gone well and I was close to 100 percent physically again. Dr. Pak was amazed by the progress I had made in such a short period of time.

"Jim, I can't believe I'm saying this," he said, "but I'm going to clear you to compete at the U.S. Open."

I was elated to hear that for a couple of reasons:

One, if he hadn't cleared me and I was injured at the Open, my health insurance wouldn't pay for it. And two, having the doctor clear me sent me a message that I was healthy enough to wrestle again. That was great news for me.

The week before the U.S. Open, I put my shoulder to its toughest test since I had been injured. I had two practice matches at the Olympic Training Center in Colorado Springs.

One was against Lindsey Durlacher and one was against Mark Rial. I was dominant in both matches.

They were both excellent young wrestlers. Durlacher went on to win a World bronze medal in 2006 and Rial won a U.S. Open title a few years later.

Wrestling those matches was very important for me. It gave me the confidence that I could make it through a match without my shoulder exploding again and that my conditioning was match ready.

## NOT ALL ROADS LEAD TO GOLD

I knew if my conditioning was good at altitude in Colorado Springs (6,000 feet about sea level) that it would be even better in a lower elevation (2,000 feet) when we competed at the U.S. Open in Las Vegas.

It was good to be able to wrestle those two matches against good opponents, but I had done no other competitive wrestling during my rehab. I was 34 years old and I knew this likely was my last realistic shot at making an Olympic Team.

Even though I had been out the entire season with an injury, I entered the U.S. Open as the No. 1 seed at 60 kilograms.

I rolled past my first three opponents to advance to the semifinals. I felt great. My shoulder was holding up well and my conditioning also felt good.

Now the matches were going to become tougher. I won a close match against a strong opponent in defeating Jacob Hey 3-1 in the semifinals. I followed by downing Glenn Nieradka 3-0 in overtime in the finals.

I won five matches and allowed a total of one point. And I had won my second straight U.S. Open title. I don't know if this qualifies as a miracle, but it must come close considering the initial diagnosis and timeline. Regardless, God still answers prayer. I did what had to be done and what some considered impossible. Everyone did their job and God provided the healing.

I felt good, but I had wrestled five matches and it took a bit of a toll on me. I did tweak my shoulder in the finals against Nieradka. I felt a little pain in the area where I had the surgery. My shoulder was sore for a couple of days, but fortunately it wasn't any more serious.

The good news was I still had six weeks before the Olympic Trials. It was nice to know that I was back and that I could start training regularly again.

Six months after a catastrophic injury that was supposed to sideline me for a year, I had moved within two wins of making my second Olympic Team.

My performance at the Open put a lot of the doubts to rest. I was back training again and back on track to making it to the

## *A path of persistence, faith and perseverance*

Olympics.

I was confident and ready headed into June's Olympic Trials at the RCA Dome in Indianapolis.

I trained with Olympic and World silver medalist Brandon Paulson prior to the Trials. It was great to work out with him. We wrestled some live matches and it was high-level competition.

He was in the weight class below me, but we still had some great battles. He's fiercely competitive, and he's strong and athletic.

Brandon was about to wrestle an epic match of his own against Dennis Hall in the 55-kilogram finals of the Olympic Trials.

I was sitting out as the other athletes in my weight class of 60 kg battled it out in the challenge tournament. Joe Warren upset Glenn Nieradka in the finals of the challenge tournament to earn a shot at me in the best-of-3 match final-round series.

Kevin Bracken, a close friend who was a weight class above me, was my main training partner at the OTC, but Joe was a close second. Unlike other athletes, I didn't avoid training against wrestlers at my weight. I had trained frequently with Joe, and I had also competed against him each several times before the 2004 Olympic Trials. I had mentored him and brought him to the 2003 World Championships as a training partner. I had the upper hand on him in all of our previous matches. I had beaten him by technical superiority a number of times, but he had been gaining ground in practice.

But that didn't mean it was going to be easy. Joe was a tenacious competitor who made me work for every point.

We had two hard-fought bouts before I was able to sweep Joe Warren in two straight matches at the Olympic Trials. I beat him 5-3 and 3-0.

We knew each other well and Joe had continued to improve. Those were tough matches against a quality opponent.

Less than eight months after having major surgery on my left shoulder, I had made my second straight Olympic Team. And I had earned the right to represent the United States at the 2004

# NOT ALL ROADS LEAD TO GOLD

Olympic Games in Athens, Greece.

This was something I had expected, but I was also relieved. It was exciting to make my second straight Olympic Team and my fifth straight U.S. World or Olympic Team overall. And thankfully this time with zero controversy.

Joe Warren went on to win a World Greco-Roman title two years later in 2006 before winning a Bellator World title in mixed martial arts.

It was interesting to see Dennis Hall make his third Olympic Team in 2004. Dennis dropped down a weight class that year. He won an incredible match against Brandon Paulson at the Olympic Trials that is still considered one of the best Greco-Roman matches of all-time.

It was a physical, hard-fought battle between World and Olympic medalists. When Hall finally emerged victorious after a marathon battle, the wrestlers hugged and the fans in Indy gave both wrestlers a well-deserved standing ovation.

We were long-time rivals, but Dennis and I were now teammates on the Olympic Team. And we actually warmed up together before we wrestled in a tune-up tournament prior to the 2004 Olympics.

I continued to progress in the time before the Olympic Games. My shoulder had healed and I was gaining valuable mat time I needed after being out for so long earlier in the season.

We arrived in Greece for the Olympics and once again it was all business for me as I prepared for another huge event. I was there to win an Olympic gold medal. And all of my focus was squarely set on achieving my long-time goal.

I did make time to attend the Opening Ceremonies of the 2004 Olympic Games in Athens. I couldn't miss out on another spectacular event where the Olympians from every country in every sport gathered before a sellout crowd of 100,000 fans. It was another amazing experience. I was proud to represent Team USA while the whole world was watching.

I made sure to stand close to our heavyweight, 2000 Olympic gold medalist Rulon Gardner, because I knew the cameras would

## *A path of persistence, faith and perseverance*

be on him. I stood close to Rulon so my family could see me on television during the NBC broadcast. It was an awesome night with an electric atmosphere. It definitely provided me with a boost heading into the competition.

During our final preparations for the Olympics, we were able to meet a man who had been the leader of our country. In 2004, former President George H.W. Bush came to our practice facility in Athens, Greece. I shook his hand and had an opportunity to talk briefly with him. He came into our facility and walked onto the mat to meet with our team.

It was very informal, but it was an amazing opportunity for us. President Bush was a big sports fan and it was very cool that he came to see us.

My training was going well and I was feeling good going into the Olympics, but I had missed significant training and competition during the time I had rehabbed. I wasn't quite as sharp as I had hoped, but under the circumstances I was still wrestling at a high level.

I wasn't even supposed to be wrestling after being told I needed a take a year off after my injury. But I was a veteran and I knew what I needed to do. I had a game plan and I was ready to go.

I weighed in and received my draw for the 2004 Olympic Games. And competition day finally arrived. I drew a familiar opponent in my first match. Hugo Passos of Portugal. I had wrestled the guy before and I had beaten him handily. I was confident I would do it again.

I was ready to go. I slapped hands with my coaches and bounced onto the mat to begin competition at my second Olympic Games.

As I reached the center of the mat, a bizarre exchange occurred. The official shook my hand and told me: "Take it easy on this guy because he's deaf."

That was the last thing I heard before my first match of the 2004 Olympics. It was an odd occurrence and I didn't react to it well. For some reason, that had a negative impact on me. It really

# NOT ALL ROADS LEAD TO GOLD

rattled me and I lost my focus.

The match started and my opponent took control. I was put down for passivity and he hit a reverse lift and threw me. He executed a five-point move and I fell behind 7-0. I was in trouble. Big trouble.

I needed to regroup quickly or he would go up by 10 points to end the match by technical superiority. Fortunately, I was able to regroup and I mounted my comeback.

I finally scored late in the first period. I was still down 7-3 to start the second period, but I had received my wake-up call and I was confident I could rally.

I went on a tear after that. I threw him twice and then turned him twice with a front headlock. The last time I got him on his back, I held him there and pinned him.

That obviously wasn't the type of match I expected, but it was the Olympic Games. There are no easy matches in the Olympics. I received a painful reminder of that in my first bout.

My next match was against a familiar opponent: Eusebiu Diaconu of Romanian. He was a wrestler I had beaten before and I was confident I could do it again.

I was scheduled to wrestle him in the bronze-medal match at the 2003 World Championships, but I couldn't wrestle him after dislocating my shoulder in the semifinals. Needless to say, I was anxious and eager to wrestle him again.

The match was scoreless after the first period. I came out aggressively, but he was blocking me and trying to slow me down. We went to the clinch to start the second period. The clinch position was where wrestlers locked their arms around each other's backs.

We locked up in the clinch and the whistle blew. And then I blew it. He threw me in the clinch for three points. I was down 3-0.

The Romanian put on the track shoes and took off running after that. I was chasing him all over the mat while trying desperately to rally.

With about a minute left in the match, I felt a sharp pain in

## A path of persistence, faith and perseverance

my hand. The Romanian had bit me. He bit me on my left hand on the big fleshy part that is right under the thumb. My hand started bleeding and I showed the referee, who was from Russia.

"He bit me!" I shouted to the official.

The referee shrugged his shoulders, smiled at me and said, "Keep wrestling."

I couldn't believe it, but it was also a Russian official. They weren't known for doing any favors for a wrestler from the United States.

Then I showed my coach, Steve Fraser, my hand and he started chirping at the officials. The referee then told Fraser to be quiet.

My opponent should have been disqualified for doing something blatantly illegal. He bit me on the hand.

Near the end of the match, I was frustrated and I ran the Romanian off the mat and they called him for fleeing the mat. They gave me a point, but it was too late for a comeback. There were just a few seconds left in the bout.

He won the match 3-1. It was devastating and frustrating. I went into that tournament with the mindset that I was going to win a medal.

I was still a little rusty from all of the time I was off the mat following my surgery. But I still felt like I could've landed a spot on the medal podium.

I had wrestled in my second Olympics and I had lost my second match. I was out of the tournament.

I ended up placing 10th at my second Olympic Games. I knew it was probably my last chance to compete in the Olympics.

I would've been 38 years old at the next Olympics in 2008 and I wasn't planning on wrestling another four years.

I took some time to ponder my future as a wrestler. I didn't want to make an emotional decision right after the Olympics.

I didn't achieve my ultimate goal, but my two trips to the Olympic Games were great experiences.

Would I do it all over again with the same results? Absolutely. if one truly believes "it's about the journey" then you

## NOT ALL ROADS LEAD TO GOLD

accept the results and appreciate how the journey molded you into a better version of yourself. I also believe that God is sovereign. There had to be a reason, one that I didn't understand at the time, but have a clearer idea now. Regardless, I needed to be grateful for what I had, rather than bitter for what I didn't have.

For 12 years, I expended what some would label as superhuman effort, but not everything turned out how I envisioned. And yet, I had the opportunity to train and compete for 12 years at the World and Olympic level. And I enjoyed every moment of it.
I dove deep into the waters of being an Olympic-level athlete.

You don't want to live for moments – you want to live in moments. I want to live in the moment for God's glory.

Everything I was able to experience was more than worth it. I didn't want to be average. I wanted to train to be extraordinary.

I didn't reach the level of Greco-Roman legends Alexander Karelin or Armen Nazaryan. But making the Olympics is something rare and extraordinary for someone to accomplish. And I made it twice.

I gave it everything I had. I really did. I truly believed being a wrestler was what I was made to do. It was a lifestyle that I loved and truly enjoyed.

I made mistakes and experienced setbacks, but each mistake and misfortune provided an opportunity to learn and grow.

It was quite a journey for an ornery kid from Wisconsin who faced his share of obstacles growing up. It was an honor to represent my country twice on the biggest stage in sports at the Olympic Games.

After I finished competing, I spent a few days exploring Greece. It's a beautiful country. My wife and family went sightseeing after the Olympics.

There is some great history in Athens and we enjoyed taking in some of the sights.

It turned out that I wasn't quite finished with wrestling. A few months after the Olympics, I competed at the Sunkist Kids International in Arizona and won the tournament.

## *A path of persistence, faith and perseverance*

I had one final moment with Team USA after the 2004 Olympics. I went to the White House again with the other Olympians.

There wasn't a whole lot of time for us in the White House, but it was still a memorable day. We came in and took a photo with President George W. Bush. I was close enough to him where I was able to shake his hand.

President Bush gave a short speech and thanked all of the Olympians for representing the U.S. in Athens.

Through wrestling, I was able to meet three U.S. Presidents and shake each of their hands. It was awesome that wrestling opened the door for those incredible opportunities.

## CHAPTER 10
# CALLED TO COACH

I had just competed for the United States at my second straight Olympic Games in 2004 in Athens, Greece. And I was still wrestling at a high level.

I had placed 10th at the Olympics after finishing fourth at the 2003 World Championships. I was 34 years old and had been wrestling on the Senior level for more than a decade. At this point, I was conflicted and uncertain. I was entering my mid 30s and was married with two kids while struggling to make ends meet. I was still chasing my goal of winning a medal at the highest level of international wrestling.

I went back to what I knew. Just a couple of months after Athens, I was back on the mat that October when I captured a Greco-Roman title at the Sunkist Kids International Open in Tempe, Arizona.

Shortly after that tournament, I was presented with a new opportunity by USA Wrestling. I was approached by U.S. National Coach Steve Fraser and U.S. National Teams Director Mitch Hull.

They asked me if I would be interested in becoming an assistant coach to Ivan Ivanov at the U.S. Olympic Education Center Greco-Roman program at Northern Michigan University.

At the time, I was finally being paid as a full-time math teacher at Hilltop Baptist School in Colorado Springs. Despite the pay raise, the job offer at the USOEC was too good of an

## NOT ALL ROADS LEAD TO GOLD

opportunity for me. Plus, I was going to be paid full-time to coach Greco-Roman wrestling. That was the perfect fit for me and seemed like an opportunity for a fresh start.

Ivan Ivanov, the USOEC's head coach, was someone that I knew well. When Dennis Hall brought Ivanov from Bulgaria to the U.S. to train in 1992, I was able to train periodically with him during his time in Wisconsin.

We competed against each other three years later. Ivanov had just won a World silver medal for Bulgaria and I had little experience on the international level. We faced off against each other at the 1995 Sweden Grand Prix with Ivan defeating me by a convincing 9-1 score.

Ten years later, Ivan became my boss when I joined the USOEC program as a full-time assistant Greco-Roman coach in 2005.

We already knew each other and had a mutual respect. I believe that enabled us to work well together as coaches.

Not only had we competed against each other, he had also helped coach me at the OTC periodically in the late 1990s when he moved to the U.S. He was helpful at a few tournaments when his USOEC coaching responsibilities put him at the same tournaments overseas or in the United States.

As I anticipated, we clicked right away when we started coaching together. We had great chemistry and we hit the ground running. We shared a similar vision and we had the same goals. We wanted to develop World and Olympic champions. We had the same goals as coaches that we had as athletes. We wanted to be No. 1. We were very motivated and we had high goals for our program.

I lived in the dormitories at Northern Michigan University for my first two months on the job before my family was able to join me in Marquette, Michigan.

Ivan brought intangibles to the wrestling room that were difficult to replicate. He has a very good understanding of Greco-Roman wrestling. He's a great technical coach – one of the best in the world. He knows the technique and also knows how to

## A path of persistence, faith and perseverance

demonstrate it. He's an outstanding teacher. It was impressive and inspiring to watch him work.

Ivanov also found ways to train his wrestlers off the mat. Ivan had so many creative ways to train his teams. The man is a cross-training genius outside of being a very good Greco coach.

I had coached just one year at the collegiate level before working under Ivanov. I was still pretty new to coaching, so when I started working with him it was an apprenticeship at first. My role eventually expanded and he started giving me more responsibility. And he started letting me run some of the practices.

Ivan was a tough, hard-nosed coach, but he was continually looking to improve and evolve. He was always open to suggestions. It was definitely his program and he was in charge. But Ivan always included me on everything and sought my input. When we did well and had success, he always made sure to credit me for our success as well. That meant a lot to me. We had great mutual respect for each other and that went a long way in the relationship we had.

We had great chemistry, but we didn't agree on everything. I believed in shorter, crisper practices, but that rarely happened under Ivanov's watch.

Ivan would have some really long practices. He would turn them into marathon, three-plus hour practices. He wasn't trying to torture you – his ultimate goal was to make you better. He wanted to coach the guys until they properly learned a technique. He spent a long time teaching a move. They understood he sincerely wanted them to improve. The results spoke for themselves.

Ivan would've stayed in the wrestling room all day if he could. That was his sanctuary. And his laboratory. He was trying to develop his wrestlers to be Olympic caliber and he invested an enormous amount of time into his craft.

During our time there, we also elevated the expectations for the Greco program at Northern Michigan. The USOEC was originally considered a developmental program for aspiring

## NOT ALL ROADS LEAD TO GOLD

Olympic athletes who were just out of high school. Once those wrestlers graduated from Northern Michigan, they were then expected to move on to train with Senior athletes at the U.S. Olympic Training Center in Colorado Springs.

It ended up not being just a developmental program when we started putting guys on Senior World teams and Olympic teams. Ivan's vision was we weren't going to take a backseat to anybody. He wanted our guys to be the best in the world.

We shared a vision of our wrestlers challenging the guys on the Senior level. We knew if that happened, we would all get better together. If you look at the U.S. results from 2004-08, it drove the American Greco program up to a very high level.

I had stopped competing, but I was still on the mat training with the USOEC athletes twice a day. I was still in excellent shape and still wrestling at a high level.

Two years after coming to Northern Michigan as a coach, I chose to return to competition in August 2007.

The U.S. fell short of placing in the top six at the 2007 World Championships at 60 kilograms (132 pounds), meaning our country had still not qualified for the 2008 Olympics in that weight class.

With three Olympic qualifiers left, and 2006 World champion Joe Warren serving a two-year suspension, the U.S. was in danger of not making the Olympics at 60 kilograms.

Warren was ranked No. 1 in the world, and his absence left a huge gap in the U.S. lineup. At one point, I told our guys if they didn't step up and fill the gap that I would come out of retirement. Their response was almost a unanimous, "Yeah, whatever old man." But eventually I made the decision to return to wrestling because the younger guys weren't getting the job done.

I called USA Wrestling Executive Director Rich Bender and U.S. National Coach Steve Fraser to tell them I was interested in coming back to wrestle. They were both supportive of the idea.

A week after I came back, I tore my MCL (medial collateral ligament) in practice. Six weeks later, I wrestled in the Sunkist Kids International Open in October 2007 in Tempe, Arizona. I

*A path of persistence, faith and perseverance*

advanced to the finals against one of the wrestlers I coached, Joe Betterman.

The match with Joe wasn't close. He took me for a ride on the Betterman Express. He started in the reverse lift position, picked me up and launched me into the parking lot. He threw me all over the arena and sent a strong message. He wasn't about to relinquish his No. 1 spot on the U.S. ladder.

In that same tournament, I also continued to coach. I sat in the corner and coached a number of the USOEC wrestlers who competed at the Sunkist event.

After the loss to Betterman, I knew I needed to make some adjustments. The rules had changed and I had to become better in the reverse lift position, especially now that each period started with the top opponent getting a free lock while the down athlete started on his hands and knees. And I had to figure out how to effectively and efficiently wrestle the one-minute period on my feet.

Even with the setback, I was still confident I could be the No. 1 guy in the United States at 60 kilos. Losing never made me want to quit wrestling. It's made me want to wrestle more. I felt like I had unfinished business and I wanted to figure out what I could do better. I was 37 years old, but I also knew making my third straight Olympic Team was a realistic goal.

Ivan was incredibly supportive of my move. I continued to coach while also still training with the athletes at the USOEC.

I wrestled again in two more tournaments – the Dave Schultz Memorial International and the Hungarian Grand Prix – and fell short of placing at both events. I had been out of competition for a while, and I wasn't sharp in either tournament. I wasn't winning, but I was making small adjustments and improvements each time.

I finally started to hit my stride when I headed to Las Vegas for the U.S. Open. I captured the U.S. Open championship in April 2008. I defeated Betterman 5-0, 8-3 in the finals at 60 kilograms.

Betterman had replaced Joe Warren in the U.S. lineup at the

## NOT ALL ROADS LEAD TO GOLD

2007 World Championships in Baku, Azerbaijan. And he had taken it to me when we had wrestled a few months before in Arizona.

It was a good sign that I had made a big progression since that setback. I had emerged as the frontrunner to make the U.S. Olympic Team at 60 kg. It was a huge swing from getting wrecked by Betterman in the Sunkist finals to beating him in the U.S. Open.

I was about to turn 38 years old, but I was feeling good and I had just turned in a strong performance. I had the inside track on being an Olympian again.

At the same time, I was a little disappointed in the guys I was coaching because I felt like they should be wrestling better. I wrestled two guys at the Open – Betterman and Willie Madison – who I coached at Northern Michigan.

Ivan was fully supportive of me returning to the mat. He felt like I was a hammer that drove guys to where they needed to be. I was an older, experienced, proven guy who could train with our guys and push them.

Shortly after I won the U.S. Nationals title, Ivanov delivered a strong and poignant message to our team at Northern Michigan.

"You see what Jim does," Ivanov said in broken English. "He wins Nationals. He is hard worker."

Ivan used what I was doing to drive our wrestlers to become better versions of themselves. I know it motivated them and pushed them. He kind of rubbed some of our wrestlers' faces in it that I had beaten them. It made it a little awkward in our wrestling room. Unfortunately, my comeback to competition was short-lived.

The first Olympic qualifier, with the Pan American countries, had already taken place in Colorado Springs. Betterman had competed and fell short of qualifying the U.S. for the Olympics.

Two weeks after winning the U.S. Open, I was sent to the second Olympic qualifier in Rome, Italy. In my first match of the tournament, I injured my shoulder early in my first match.

## *A path of persistence, faith and perseverance*

My opponent was in the top position. He turned me with a gut-wrench and my elbow hit the mat. My forearm got stuck in the mat and I dislocated my left shoulder again. And I tore my labrum.

Once again, I was in excruciating pain. And it was worse this time because I knew it was career-ending. This was going to be the last time I wrestled a competitive match. It was a tough way to finish.

It was almost the same exact injury I had suffered at the 2003 World Championships. I had another surgery, and I had another four titanium anchors put in. Four of the five anchors from the first surgery had been torn free from the ligament when I reinjured my shoulder in Rome.

I had no regrets about deciding to make a comeback, but definitely had a feeling of disappointment.

I had come back and won the U.S. Open. I came back after almost three years off and won a national title. I came away with something. I had come out of retirement to try and help my country land a spot in the Olympic Games.

I thought I was the best guy for the job and I proved that at the Open. You can't regret doing the right thing, and what I did was the right thing.

I was done wrestling, but I continued to coach full-time at the U.S. Olympic Education Center at Northern Michigan. When I returned to practice, the depth that Ivan Ivanov had built at Northern Michigan was evident during our grueling practice sessions.

We had great competition in the wrestling room. It was awesome. Guys fed off each other. Ivan liked creating that competition in the room. It was a challenging environment. If you didn't like where you were standing in line, get better. He was trying to motivate guys and it worked.

As tough and demanding as he could be in the wrestling room, Ivan was just as caring and compassionate off the mat.

Ivan created a really good family environment at Northern Michigan. He would have the team over to his house and cook us

# NOT ALL ROADS LEAD TO GOLD

shish kabob. He took care of the guys who wrestled for him. He treated them like they were his sons. He created an environment where the wrestlers would do anything for him. Even after guys graduated, they didn't want to go to Colorado Springs to the Olympic Training Center. They loved Ivan and wanted to wrestle for him. They would run through the brick wall in the room for Ivan.

As nice and as beloved as Ivan was by his athletes, he didn't make it easy on them. Ivan could definitely test their patience with those three-hour practices. He also could upset guys when it got competitive when he wrestled with them in practice. He would push guys, and push them to their limits. He challenged the athletes because he wanted them to reach their full potential.

Ivan was much more of an old school coach than I was, but we complemented each other well in the corner when coaching during an event.

Ivan was more direct and intense – and not the most tactful sometimes with the wrestlers. A lot of that was from the way he was coached in Bulgaria. His coaches were hard-nosed, no-nonsense and direct. That's how he was trained.

I was more encouraging and understanding sometimes to balance what he was doing. He was definitely old school and I used a little bit different approach. It worked well for us. The wrestlers responded well to it.

During my time at Northern Michigan, we were able to develop a number of wrestlers who went on to excel on the Senior level.

One of those wrestlers was Spenser Mango, who made U.S. Olympic Teams in 2008 and 2012. I spent a lot of time with Spenser, and we wrestled with each other quite a bit. I spent a significant number of hours training with him. He was very close to winning medals at the World and Olympic medal.

He was an explosive and dynamic wrestler who was very strong for his size. Spenser was a high character guy and just someone you loved to coach.

One of the most talented Greco-Roman wrestlers I've ever

## A path of persistence, faith and perseverance

been around was Harry Lester. Harry was a dynamic and explosive wrestler who won two World bronze medals and made the 2012 Olympic Team.

Harry should've been a World champion. He was the best wrestler on the planet in 2007, but there were a few interesting calls that went against him at the World Championships.

Harry got robbed in that tournament. They stopped the match while Harry was pinning the guy from Azerbaijan in the semifinals. The match was in Azerbaijan and they cheated to help their guy win. Harry should have won that match and should have been a World champion. It was horrible what the officials did to him in that match. They definitely robbed Harry of a gold medal.

Harry was a part of the U.S. squad that captured the team title at the 2007 World Championships. It's the only time in U.S. history that an American team has won Worlds in Greco-Roman wrestling.

Harry trained hard in the room. He didn't always follow the plan the coaches had for him. But he was a tremendous talent. He was an exciting and explosive wrestler. No doubt, he should have been a World and Olympic champion.

Adam Wheeler was another guy who made great improvements during his time at the USOEC. He never made a World Team, but he won an Olympic bronze medal for the United States in 2008.

Adam wasn't a superstar athlete, but he was a hard worker and he got hot at the right time. He wrestled well at the Olympic Trials and kept it going at the Olympics. It was a storybook finish for him at the Olympics.

He did virtually everything right. He worked hard, he listened to the coaches and he bought into what we were doing. He did an outstanding job.

Andy Bisek was another wrestler who was very raw when he joined the program at Northern Michigan as a walk-on. Andy made tremendous gains during his time at the USOEC. He went on to win two World bronze medals, in 2014 and 2015, and make the 2016 U.S. Olympic Team. He then went on to coach at

## NOT ALL ROADS LEAD TO GOLD

Northern Michigan.

Andy was very similar to Adam Wheeler. He bought into the plan and was a super hard worker. He trained for a number of years at Northern Michigan and he continued to improve every year. He stayed in the Greco-Roman system for many years. Andy wasn't a superstar, but he was a tough, hard-nosed grinder who had a heck of a career.

2012 Olympian Chas Betts was another wrestler who worked extremely hard during his time with Ivan and me at Northern Michigan.

Chas has gone on to a successful career with World Wrestling Entertainment. He has become hugely popular while wrestling under the names Chad Gable and Shorty G.

Chas was another guy who wasn't necessarily a superstar. He worked super hard. I have nothing but good things to say about him. He was very coachable and he was a tough competitor. He wasn't afraid to wrestle anybody.

I left Northern Michigan shortly before Ivan Ivanov did in 2009. I accepted a position as the head coach at Wheaton College, a Christian school in suburban Chicago.

I still incorporate many of the things that Ivan did at Northern Michigan into what I do as a head coach. And I have an abundance of Ivan stories that I share with my college wrestlers.

I love Ivan Ivanov – he's a wonderful human being. He's a very intelligent, caring, passionate and driven man who is just a genuinely great guy. He's been hugely successful in his life and his career. I certainly enjoyed my time with him. He's had an incredible impact on so many people, including me. We had some great years when we coached together. We worked well together and I enjoyed working with him.

My years at Northern Michigan were memorable and we were able to accomplish a great deal. I have fond memories from those days.

## CHAPTER 11
# PULLUPS AND PERSISTENCE

One of the best parts about being a college wrestling coach is I have no excuse for not staying in shape. I have access to all kinds of exercise equipment. And I can train and wrestle with my team at Wheaton College any time I want to.

In addition to going out onto the mat and wrestling with them, I also do strength and conditioning workouts with my team.

One workout that had been a staple for me since I first started wrestling has been pullups. It was an activity most kids did in physical education class where you would pull yourself up with your arms until your chin went up and over the bar.

I had spent decades working on an ambitious goal of doing 100 pullups in a row without stopping. Throughout the 1990s and early 2000s, when I was competing in college and then internationally, I always had the goal of reaching 100 pullups. I had come close, but I kept falling short. My record was 95.

My goal of 100 pullups was put on hold when I had shoulder surgery during the 2008 Olympic year after I had briefly returned to competition. I eventually starting doing pullups again to help rehabilitate my shoulder in 2009.

I was working at a wrestling camp in Michigan in the summer of 2009 and one of the kids asked me if I could do 100 pullups. I decided I was going to make a run at my long-time goal.

With all of the kids watching and cheering me on, I did 101

## NOT ALL ROADS LEAD TO GOLD

pullups without stopping in 2009. It was crazy. They shot a video of it, so there is actual proof that I finally achieved my goal.

When I took the head coaching job at Wheaton, I was doing a strength and conditioning workout in the weight room.

I was chirping at my wrestlers about how a 40-year-old man with two shoulder surgeries could do more pullups than they could. A couple of the wrestlers asked me, "How many pullups can you do?"

Determined not to be shown up, I jumped to the bar and did 107 consecutive pullups. It was my second year at Wheaton in the fall of 2010.

It was something we had fun with. And I hope it inspired the guys to see their 40-something year-old coach doing pullups.

I love training alongside my wrestlers. It motivates them and pushes them. Plus, it allows me to stay in shape. I jokingly tell them, even if they don't love me for the workouts that I put them through, doing it with them makes them hate me less.

The more practical reason is that I have to stay in shape. My youngest child was only 5 years old in 2020, so I need to make sure I'm around for a while to support her and watch her grow up. I'm retired from competition, but I still love to work out. And I have a regular workout routine that I follow. I honestly don't want to look her grandfather as her high school or college graduation.

This is what my typical week looks like:

Monday: Squats and dead lift in the morning for my legs. Wrestle with my college team in the afternoon.

Tuesday: Bench press for my arms in the morning with weights up to 300 pounds. Wrestling with the team in the afternoon.

Wednesday: Bulgarian Bag workout in the morning. Upper Torso Egometer or AirDyn in the afternoon.

Thursday: Pullups in the morning. Wrestle with the team in the afternoon

Friday: Chiropractor in the morning. Wrestling in the afternoon.

If we are traveling, I will find a fitness center in the hotel and

## A path of persistence, faith and perseverance

run a mile and a half on Friday night.

Saturday morning after weigh-ins: Upper body weight workout before competition starts.

Sunday: Day off.

It is supremely important for me to rest and recover on Sundays. It gives my body and my mind a break. Fundamentally, the belief is a part of my Christian worldview that believes God mandates we work for six days and rest for one. Sunday is culturally easiest and works well with the Wheaton schedule. And then Monday morning hits and I start up all over again.

I'm still as competitive as ever. I love to be in the profession I am in. I need to be in the environment I am in. I am very competitive in so many aspects of my life.

I love coaching at Wheaton College. I completed my 12th season as Wheaton's head coach during the 2020-21 season.

We've had our share of success stories, on and off the mat. Wheaton has had 21 national qualifiers and eight All-Americans during my time as head coach. We've also had a number of Academic All-Americans.

Wheaton is a great school, and it's academically challenging. I really enjoy working with the young men in our program.

We compete at the NCAA Division III level, meaning we are not allowed to award athletic scholarships. Wheaton is a private Christian school that is fairly expensive to attend.

We also don't have a huge budget for our wrestling program. I have one part-time, paid assistant coach along with two to four volunteer assistants.

There are 117 Division III wrestling programs nationwide and it's difficult for athletes to qualify for the national tournament. Our regional tournament has 18 teams and only the top three athletes in each weight class make it to nationals.

Less than 20 percent of the wrestlers in Division III make it to nationals. Nearly 50 percent of the wrestlers at the NCAA Division I level qualify for nationals.

Even though there are no athletic scholarships awarded in DIII, our level for wrestling is still highly competitive. A number

## NOT ALL ROADS LEAD TO GOLD

of our DIII wrestlers have proven through tournaments such as the Midlands that they can compete against DI athletes.

I really enjoy coaching at this level – it's rewarding to be able to mentor a young man and help them develop as a person. But we also face our share of challenges and obstacles.

I was asked during an interview one time if the disappointments are worse now as a coach than they were as an athlete.

I truly believe it's harder to be a coach than it is to be an athlete. It's an emotional roller-coaster. As an athlete, you can do something. You can burn off a lot of those emotions. It sucks to lose and I hated it. After I lost, I'd go and find kind of a cold, dark place because it felt like a part of me had died. That's how much it hurt to lose. I would cry like a little kid who just had his favorite toy destroyed. There were a few people who saw that, but not a lot of people did. Those moments were cathartic, and then it was over. Then I could just hit the reset button and I could go back and remember that pain, and I hated it. It would make me train a little bit harder, it would make me do a little bit more. It made me want to outwork everyone around me.

But as a coach? There isn't the same safety valve to be able to vent or get calm. So much of the emotional strain stays within. This is the brutal unspoken side of coaching. And you definitely cannot take it home because of the disruption to your family.

But as far as the disappointment? I can't be disappointed in guys who are laying it on the line out there. I may be disappointed that they lost, but I'm never disappointed in them. The same philosophy guided me as an athlete. I was never really disappointed in myself, it's more that I was disappointed in the results. I very definitely try to lead a life of no regrets. I wanted to leave it all out on the mat and my guys see what I preach and they buy into it. I believe I have captured their hearts and their minds. Not for me, but in the sense that the same faith that drove me drives them.

As previously mentioned, coaching is an emotional roller-coaster and you've got no real way of burning off those emotions

## A path of persistence, faith and perseverance

the way you did as an athlete. I've gotten to the point now where I've got to get a workout in either before a tournament or after. I have to do something just to get that out of my system. I need to have that same cathartic closure, because if you don't, it will just chew you up inside.

That's one of the awful things about being a coach. It's awesome being a coach, but you are always judged on other people's performances. You could be the greatest coach in the world and your guys have a bad day or a bad weekend, and then all of the sudden you have alumni or your superiors wondering, "Why aren't you performing, why aren't your guys performing?"

When you know you've done just about everything right, sometimes an athlete just had a bad day or something bad happened at home. Or they got sick or didn't finish an assignment. Or they had a relationship that went sideways. That's the hardest thing about being a coach – you are judged on the performance of 18-to-22- year-old young men who are notorious for making bad decisions.

But it's also rewarding when you can take someone and you can give them a vision so far beyond what they had for themselves. That's one of the joys I think working at the Division III level is that you can give them a vision they may not have for themselves. You can paint them a picture and get them to buy into it, and that's awesome. I'm sure DI coaches do the same thing – they will paint their guys a picture of being a couple-time DI national champ. Or you paint a picture of something beyond college wrestling. I heard Iowa coach Tom Brands talking about how he's looking for guys who want to be World and Olympic champions, and I think that's awesome.

Making the transition from athlete to coach was a smooth one for me. I felt like it fit me like a glove. I've always been one to encourage people to make them better. And that is essentially what it comes down to as a coach – you're trying to make people better versions of themselves.

I like to define people by their character: who they are physically, intellectually, emotionally and spiritually.

## NOT ALL ROADS LEAD TO GOLD

My job is to make the guys I coach better in all areas of their lives.

I can't focus on one thing. You can't compartmentalize your character. You can't compartmentalize who you are. You've seen guys jacked out of their minds. They're huge, they're awesome physical specimens. They look like a Greek god in a singlet; but when they get into emotionally difficult situations they crumble because they can't handle the pressure. Or they are as dumb as a box of rocks, and dumb wrestlers get beat. I'm not saying you have to be a straight-A student, but you still have to have a wrestling intelligence.

Part of what helped me make World and Olympic Teams, when surrounded by better athletes, was moral decisions. How can an elite athlete expect to grow or be able to push themselves to new heights coming to a morning practice on four hours of sleep smelling like a brewery? Again, you cannot compartmentalize character – if one part is bad it will rot the whole.

Even as a younger athlete, when I was in high school and had a high school coach, I would take the time and explain things to people. I always felt like my lot in life was to make the people around me better. It seemed natural to me to become a coach.

I taught high school math for 12 years. When you teach high school math, if you don't do it the right way, you lose your kids. You have to break things down. Being a high school math teacher really helped me become a much better coach because it helped me break things down and not assume that people know what I'm talking about, or assume that people know a position. Breaking down technique can be challenging for gifted wrestlers. They may be able to come in, do a clinic, and show some technique, but they don't know how to coach.

There is a significant difference between putting on a technique show of your best stuff and breaking down the nuances and minutia of a move so an athlete can mentally digest the information. And then create the mind and muscle memory for matches.

You have to be able to have the mindset of, "I'm here to

## A path of persistence, faith and perseverance

make these guys better versions of themselves." Much of that is the technique and you have to break it down for them in a way they can understand it.

Being a high school math teacher really helped with that. And it was my high school principal, Carl Adams, who delivered a message to me when I was fresh out of college and started teaching:

"Jim, you work really well with gifted students. Now you have to start looking to work well with the average and below-average students."

And it hit me. He was right. I'm doing these kids a disservice. I have to be a teacher for everybody, and I learned to break things down.

In my wrestling room, there are guys who don't need as much of my time. The guys who need a lot of my time aren't the superstars. Those other guys are going to be All-Americans whether you're there or not. They just need you to run the wet stone over the blade to keep the rust off, to keep them sharp and keep them accountable. The weaker guys are the ones who need the coach. Some of them might have needs that are emotional and I've got to be there for them. Or, they are weak intellectually and I need to be there for them. Or it could be physical and you need to fine-tune something. Or, it could be spiritually. They think they can be as immoral as they want and don't think it will affect their wrestling, but it does.

As a coach, especially at the DIII level, I'm not dealing with too many superstars in the room. I'm there to help make them better versions of themselves. And because of it, we all get better as a team. That's kind of the way I've looked at coaching.

We've all faced our share of adversity in this sport, and we were all forced to deal with the unfortunate circumstances that unfolded near the end of the 2019-20 wrestling season.

Like nearly everyone, we were significantly impacted by the COVID-19 Pandemic in 2020.

My Wheaton College team was set to compete at the NCAA Division III Championships, scheduled for March 13-14, 2020 in

## NOT ALL ROADS LEAD TO GOLD

Cedar Rapids, Iowa.

We had qualified one wrestler, sophomore 141-pounder Ethan Harsted, for the national tournament. Ethan turned in a strong performance to place third at the Upper Midwest Regionals and earn a berth at nationals.

Unfortunately, Ethan suffered a knee injury three days before the national tournament. He hurt his knee in the last five minutes of practice on the Tuesday before the event. We were scheduled to leave for Iowa the following day.

I was heartbroken for Ethan. He had worked hard and did a great job at our regional. We grieved with him and supported him through the process. Fortunately, he has two more years of eligibility remaining.

Just when we thought the week couldn't have become any worse, the events of March 12 unfolded. Even with Ethan out, I still traveled to Cedar Rapids for the national tournament. I had duties to perform as the President-elect of NCAA Division III wrestling.

We were still on course to hold the tournament, but on the evening of March 11 the National Basketball Association suspended play when one of its players tested positive for the virus.

And then the dominoes started to fall. The following afternoon, the NCAA announced it was cancelling all of its winter and spring championships. The NCAA Division I, II and III wrestling tournaments were cancelled.

Less than an hour after our NCAA meeting, where we were told the event was going to be held, I received the bad news via a text message at 3:45 on Thursday afternoon. I was driving back to the Marriott hotel in Cedar Rapids when I was notified.

We were less than 20 hours away from the start of our wrestling competition when the event was cancelled. All of the teams were in Cedar Rapids and the athletes were just a few hours from weigh-ins.

My first reaction as a coach was shock and disappointment. I felt really bad for the athletes and all of the work they had put in.

## A path of persistence, faith and perseverance

It was a crushing blow for a lot of people. There was frustration and anger.

Despite being upset, I realized that there was a bigger picture. How important is the NCAA tournament in the grand scheme of things? We didn't know how serious this health situation was or was going to be.

The events of March 12 impacted everyone in the sport. I witnessed grown men who have been coaching for 20 or 30 years that were really struggling emotionally.

They had invested so much time and effort into their seasons and then they were told the biggest event of the year wasn't going to happen. It obviously was a very difficult situation especially considering some of their identity is wrapped so closely with their coaching prowess.

As heartbreaking as Ethan's injury was, the moment prepared me to help others. I had already cycled through the five stages of grief several times and was in a better place emotionally to walk other coaches and athletes through the cycle. My mind was racing during the 3½-hour drive home.

As the leader of our program, I knew I needed to respond appropriately and use this as a teaching moment for our athletes, but also for the greater number of DIII coaches and athletes. I sat down immediately after I got home and wrote a letter that I emailed to all of the Division III coaches.

Here is the email I sent to the them:

*Men,*

*Many of you are hurting right now. Frustrated. Tears. Anger. Some went through this two weeks ago when an athlete didn't make it to the Nationals. I went through it two days ago when my only national qualifier injured his knee during the last five minutes of practice – he is having surgery tomorrow. But that is wrestling, we get winning and losing. We get injuries. We know that upsets happen and injuries happen. We comfort our guys and move on – this is part of coaching.*

*Yet, when a small faceless group makes a decision to end the season the day before wrestling begins, the frustration and*

## NOT ALL ROADS LEAD TO GOLD

*subsequent anger is based on a helplessness that goes well beyond the unwanted but understandable 'bad to terrible' moments of wrestling. This is next level frustration and anger.*

*When my guy was hurting, he cried, and as I held him, I let him know that I believed in him. I believed in him and his ability to get beyond this terrible moment because he is more than a wrestler and more than nationals.*

*My encouragement to you is this. Do not let this moment rob you of the joy of coaching. This is a big moment. Possibly the biggest moment of your coaching career. How will you respond to something totally out of your control? Your athletes are watching you and their response will be yours but scaled in degree. If you respond in anger, they will rage. Use this as a teaching moment. Comfort them, encourage them.*

*I believe in you because most, if not all of you, love your guys as if they are your own sons. I believe in you because you are more than the national tournament. You are coaches and mentors. You are the father to the fatherless, you are builders of men. You are awesome!*

*Jim*

Ultimately, my message to was that we can't let one bad moment rob us of the season we had. There was so much for all of us to consider after the heartbreaking and unexpected end to our season. Was the year of training worth it even if you don't compete in a national tournament or get another year back? I believe it was. If you really believe that the journey has value then even the unexpected and bad moments have value. And provide opportunities to grow and learn.

If there is some way that I can get the athletes another year back, absolutely I will help them with that. But there are so many variables that come into play. This whole situation is unprecedented. We can't react to things emotionally. We have to react intellectually. What is the best-case scenario for most athletes in this difficult situation?

Obviously, all of those factors need to be considered. We just have to move forward the best we can. Eventually, the NCAA

## A path of persistence, faith and perseverance

decided to make the 2020-21 athletic season a "free" season, meaning it would not count against their athletic eligibility.

The decision is great on the surface, but my fear was that the NCAA could also use this to cancel championship events again. As the Covid pandemic continued to be an issue, the NCAA once again chose not to hold the Division III Championships in 2021. It didn't come as a huge surprise, but again was disappointing for our team to miss out on that opportunity.

## CHAPTER 12
# FAITH AND FAMILY

Anyone who knows me is aware I have a strong faith. My faith is something I enjoy sharing with those interested in listening to what I have learned from the Bible.

I realize that it isn't for everyone – each person is entitled to their own beliefs, and I am very respectful of that. However, I believe we were created to glorify God and commanded to love Him and our neighbor. And the best way to accomplish that is to share Christ.

The place where I coach wrestling, Wheaton College, is a Christian Liberal Arts institution. It's an amazing place with strong values and an excellent academic reputation. It's a great school. And it's the perfect fit for me as someone who loves wrestling, enjoys teaching and has a strong faith. The close relationships I've developed with my athletes are priceless.

For me, my faith is what drove me as an athlete and drove my wrestling career to a great degree. It frames who I am. I didn't want my identity to be wrapped up as being just a wrestler. I wanted my identity to be wrapped up in something that is more meaningful and greater than wrestling. I think you can be a man of faith and a successful wrestler. The two are not mutually exclusive.

Two great examples would be Ben and John Peterson. They did it far better than I did. They are emblematic of the ideal Christian wrestler as Olympic gold medalists with decades of

## NOT ALL ROADS LEAD TO GOLD

proven steadfast and strong faith. Others such as Olympic and World champions Jordan Burroughs and Kyle Snyder are steadily developing the same reputation.

I developed a strong faith at an early age. It carried over into my time at Maranatha Baptist Bible College. And it has continued as an adult in my role as a husband, father, coach and mentor.

I'm actively involved in the Fellowship of Christian Athletes. I frequently give speeches to groups that center around my faith.

You can often see me wearing a T-shirt with the words "Jesus Christ is Life" in big letters on it.

It's accompanied by the Bible verse from Philippians 1:21:

"To live is Christ and to die is gain."

The principle of the verse proclaims how we should live our life and there are greater gains being in Heaven.

Before that time comes, our purpose on Earth is to live as a light of hope in the darkness of sin and death. We live a life of sacrifice so we may be assured that even our death will glorify Christ Jesus.

I am a Christian. I have a relationship with God through Christ. One of my favorite mantras is: Jesus Christ is Life. The Rest is Just Wrestling.

Another one is: Seek Perfection. Settle for Excellence.

My identity isn't wrapped up in wrestling. It's something far greater than that. I am much more than wrestling.

The lessons I've learned have shaped me and God has used that as a tool that makes me who I am. My value isn't wrapped up in my wins and losses. We take comfort in knowing life is much bigger than us.

You can sum the Bible up with, "Love God and love your neighbor." That is the message I follow in my life.

We get so wrapped up in winning and losing. It should be about what lessons you learn. Being a man of faith has helped me deal with the highs and lows. It kept me from becoming arrogant in the high moments and from becoming despondent in the low moments.

Philippians 4:13 is a perfect example of this, yet also one of

## *A path of persistence, faith and perseverance*

the most misused verses in the Bible. "I can do all things through Christ who strengthens me." I am not able to rip a full-grown oak tree out of the ground or win Olympic gold because of the misuse of a Bible verse. The real meaning in the context of the passage is that I have the strength to handle life through Christ.

I don't use my faith as a sledgehammer. I don't push it onto people. But it's a strong presence in who I am. It has to be.

I have read the entire Bible more than 20 times. I read the Bible and pray each morning for about 30-60 minutes after I wake up.

I've been asked how I reconcile being a person of faith and also being able to turn it on as ferocious competitor. Wrestling is a violent sport, but it's an art as well. It's a martial art.

If you look at Jesus Christ, he was super intense. He was the ultimate example of fierce and compassionate. The fierce gentleman. Grace and truth. Power and direction. Power without direction is destructive and direction without power goes nowhere. I can be a super intense wrestler and still have a strong faith.

For me, that was simple. There are rules in our sport and I never stepped across any lines. Now, I'm going to be very blunt. One time I walked off the mat and I was with 2008 Olympian T.C. Dantzler, and he said to me, "Wow, you are such a dick when you wrestle." His words. At first, I was like, "What? It's not like I'm doing anything illegal." He said to me, "No, you're not, you're just a hard-nosed wrestler and you just want to crush your opponent." It's a fight, right? Wrestling is a fight. It's a martial art, but it has rules. I wrestled guys who thumbed me in the eyeballs, I've had guys bite me or grab my crotch. I had guys do cheap stuff to me. I had my head split 13, 14 times from guys headbutting me and I'm getting stitches. I never did that to my opponents. But I could still put the hurt on them.

And the reason I can do that, and how I reconcile that, is I wrestle within the rules. There is also nothing within the rules that contradicts the Christian faith. There's nothing wrong with it, and I look to Christ, which is who I'm told to frame my life after and follow. He was a very intense individual. If He could be intense the

## NOT ALL ROADS LEAD TO GOLD

way he was supposed to be, then I can be intense within the sport of wrestling.

I think if anything, my faith made me stronger because it drove me. I wanted to be as tough as Christ, and toughness isn't what you can dish out, toughness is what you can endure. The toughest thing I've ever done was after I dislocated my shoulder at the 2003 World Championships. I came back 5½ months later for the U.S. Open after being in a sling for six weeks. That was the most I ever had to endure in wrestling. That experience is nothing compared to what Christ endured on His way and on the cross.

Giving out a beating isn't tough – it just means you're better than the other guy. Going through that brutal six months, that was hell, or at least as close as I ever want to get to it. I don't think there is anything at all as a man of faith, as a Christian, that says I can't be tough, rugged, and brutal when I'm wrestling so long as I don't step across those lines where it's illegal.

Wrestling is such a physical sport and I did it as fiercely as I could. You can be a kind, compassionate person off the mat and still be a tenacious competitor on the mat.

I couldn't show any weakness on the mat. When I stepped on the mat, I showed strength. There was only one will greater than mine and that was God's will. I wanted people to walk off the mat thinking they could never beat me. Ever.

I remember for most of my career, not only wanting to win but wanting to be voted the Outstanding Wrestler. I remember praying most if not every time for that recognition – that glory.

There is nothing wrong with wanting to be the best, but who are we pointing to when we are the best? Who is getting the glory? God is to be glorified with the gifts he has given us.

In James 4:10, it says, "Humble yourselves before the Lord, and he will lift you up." Becoming a Christian was the best decision I ever made. It's shaped me into the person I've become.

I celebrated my 50th birthday in the summer of 2020, but I haven't slowed down much over the years. Reading the story of the folk hero John Henry as a kid has never left me – it compelled me to work so hard my heart exploded. To die for a worthy cause for

## *A path of persistence, faith and perseverance*

something you believe in. But even John Henry isn't mankind's savior. Christ took that mission to the next level. If one day, I strain so hard I die in service to Him, what is the downside? Heaven? There is no downside. The Disciples understood that post-resurrection.

I'm still trying to crush Ivan Ivanov's Bulgarian Bag workouts and seeing if I can crank out more pullups than my college wrestlers. I'm still very competitive. I set goals and push myself to achieve them. That's just my nature. I'm always striving to do something that takes a great commitment and focus.

My life definitely keeps me busy. I continue to coach full-time at Wheaton College, and I'm also busy with wrestling camps during the summer.

My wife, Rachel, and I are blessed to have seven amazing children in our lives. My wife is incredible in every way. I hit the jackpot when I married her. She's the best. I'm so thankful she's in my life.

On our 23rd anniversary, in 2020, I reflected on how fortunate I was to marry her. The Bible verse of Proverbs 31:29 captures my feelings for Rachel perfectly:

"Many women have done wonderful things, but you surpass them all."

Marrying her was one of the best decisions I ever made. And I can still make her laugh. She's the perfect partner for me on this journey and she's been an excellent mother for our children.

If you look at the inconsistency of my wrestling before I got married and the consistency after, you can make a strong conclusion that our marriage made me a better man and a better wrestler.

I found a partner who I loved unconditionally. I had that consistency and stability in my life. I needed that. I had other relationships that didn't work out and I think it had a negative impact on my wrestling.

They were the wrong relationships at the wrong time. Rachel was the right relationship at the right time.

Her world was turned upside when she married this hyper,

## NOT ALL ROADS LEAD TO GOLD

high-energy young guy who competed in a combat sport.

She didn't grow up in the same highly competitive world that I did. She hadn't been around it and it was overwhelming for her at times.

Regardless, she navigated those waters with me and having Rachel there was hugely important for me. I always knew I had her support. There was a definite comfort level for me when she was at my tournaments.

Rachel didn't know much about wrestling. All I know is when she came into the picture, I became much more successful as a wrestler. The results speak for themselves. I knew regardless of my results that she would still love me.

For me, my top priorities are faith and family. Wrestling is a distant third, but it's still important for me.

I am so fortunate and blessed that Rachel came into my life. And the timing couldn't have been better. She's an amazing woman.

Rachel and I have a son, Adin, and six daughters, Arwyn, Ava, Autumn, Aleyse, Ashley and Amber.

We started with Adin because it was the only name we could agree on. As a Lord of the Rings nerd, Arwyn was our choice for the next child and then we liked Ava.

At that point, we realized we had chosen three names that started with an 'A' and were two syllables – so we just went with that.

I love my God and am thankful for the life and the family He has blessed me with. I aspire to live my life to the fullest and I try to make the most of every day I am blessed to have.

It's been an incredible journey and I'm excited to see what lies ahead in the years that follow. I learned long ago that it isn't about the results, but the journey and the development.

Not all roads lead to gold. I talked about that in a speech I wrote in 2020 for the Fellowship of Christian Athletes.

There are 330 athletes who qualify each year for the NCAA Division I wrestling tournament. Only 80 of the 330 will become All-Americans. That's less than 25 percent who reach the medal

## A path of persistence, faith and perseverance

podium. Only 10 wrestlers will walk away with no disappointment. Only 10 of the 330 win a national title.

Are the 320 who didn't win going to regret they didn't win gold? Or are they are going to appreciate the journey they were on?

Very few people are going to reach the pinnacle. If you don't reach the top, is everything you've done to that point worthless? I don't believe that. There are so few people who become the very best at what they do.

Maybe they didn't win a gold medal, but because of what they learned in wrestling it has helped them go on to successful lives and careers.

Through their wrestling experiences, they developed a strong work ethic and they learned how to cope with adversity.

I made two Olympic Teams and three World Teams, but fell short of my goal of winning a medal for the United States. But, if I could, I would still go back and do it all over again.

I've still had my share of memorable experiences in life. And I have certainly learned many valuable lessons along the way.

In the end, not all roads lead to gold. But with the right perspective, and the lessons learned, the journey traveled is definitely golden.